PLOUGHSHARES

Fall 2012 • Vol. 38, Nos. 2&3

GUEST EDITOR
Patricia Hampl

EDITOR-IN-CHIEF
Ladette Randolph

MANAGING EDITOR
Andrea Martucci

FICTION EDITOR
Margot Livesey

POETRY EDITOR
John Skoyles

FOUNDING EDITOR
DeWitt Henry

FOUNDING PUBLISHER
Peter O'Malley

PRODUCTION MANAGER
Akshay Ahuja

EDITORIAL ASSISTANT
Abby Travis

SENIOR READERS
Sarah Banse, David Goldstein,
Wesley Rothman & Abby Travis

INTERNS
Belle Cushing, Jennifer Feinberg,
& Jordan Stillman

COPY EDITOR
Carol Farash

ePUBLISHING CONSULTANT
John Rodzvilla

DIGITAL PUBLICATION ASSISTANT
Jessica Arnold

READERS
Kristin George Bagdanov | Jana Lee Balish | Rowan E. Beaird
Mary Kovaleski Byrnes | Doug Paul Case | Anne Champion
Elizabeth Christensen | Marlena Clark | Susannah Clark | Lindsay D'Andrea
Ricky Davis | Nicole DiCello | Diana Filar | Colleen Fullin | Joshua Garstka
Bethany Gordon | Kristine Greive | Adam Hanover | Amanda Hartzell
Mark Hengstler | Anna Hofvander | Ethan Joella | Jocelyn Kerr | Eson Kim
Jordan Koluch | Aaron Krol | Karen Lonzo | Alexis Mackintosh-Zebrowski
LuzJennifer Martinez | Jean Mattes | Autumn McClintock | Leslie McIntyre
Stephanie Mendoza | Eileen Mullan | Kathleen Perruzzi | Miranda Roberson
June Rockefeller | M. Austen Roe | Erin Salada | Nick Sansone
Ellen Scheuermann | Mallory Schwan | Charlotte Seley | Alessandra Siraco
Katherine Sticca | Sebastian Stockman | Kristen Sund | Jessica Survelas
Regina Tavani | Angela Voras-Hills | Caitlin Walls | Leah Welch | Caitlin White

ADVISORY BOARD
William H. Berman | DeWitt Henry | Alice Hoffman | Ann Leary
Tom Martin | Pam Painter | Janet Silver | Daniel Tobin | Marillyn Zacharis

Ploughshares, a journal of new writing, is guest-edited serially by prominent writers who explore different and personal visions, aesthetics, and literary circles. *Ploughshares* is published in April, August, and December at Emerson College, 120 Boylston Street, Boston, MA 02116-4624. Telephone: (617) 824-3757. Web address: pshares.org. E-mail: pshares@pshares.org.

Advisory Editors: Sherman Alexie, Russell Banks, Andrea Barrett, Charles Baxter, Ann Beattie, Madison Smartt Bell, Anne Bernays, Frank Bidart, Amy Bloom, Robert Boswell, Henry Bromell, Rosellen Brown, Ron Carlson, James Carroll, David Daniel, Madeline DeFrees, Mark Doty, Rita Dove, Stuart Dybek, Cornelius Eady, Martín Espada, B. H. Fairchild, Nick Flynn, Carolyn Forché, Richard Ford, George Garrett, Lorrie Goldensohn, Mary Gordon, Jorie Graham, David Gullette, Marilyn Hacker, Donald Hall, Joy Harjo, Kathryn Harrison, Stratis Haviaras, Terrance Hayes, DeWitt Henry, Edward Hirsch, Jane Hirshfield, Tony Hoagland, Alice Hoffman, Fanny Howe, Marie Howe, Gish Jen, Justin Kaplan, Bill Knott, Yusef Komunyakaa, Maxine Kumin, Don Lee, Philip Levine, Margot Livesey, Thomas Lux, Gail Mazur, Campbell McGrath, Heather McHugh, James Alan McPherson, Sue Miller, Lorrie Moore, Paul Muldoon, Antonya Nelson, Jay Neugeboren, Howard Norman, Tim O'Brien, Joyce Peseroff, Carl Phillips, Jayne Anne Phillips, Robert Pinsky, Alberto Ríos, Lloyd Schwartz, Jim Shepard, Jane Shore, Charles Simic, Gary Soto, Elizabeth Spires, David St. John, Maura Stanton, Gerald Stern, Mark Strand, Elizabeth Strout, Christopher Tilghman, Richard Tillinghast, Colm Tóibín, Chase Twichell, Jean Valentine, Fred Viebahn, Ellen Bryant Voigt, Dan Wakefield, Derek Walcott, Rosanna Warren, Alan Williamson, Eleanor Wilner, Tobias Wolff, C. D. Wright, Al Young, Kevin Young

Subscriptions (ISSN 0048-4474): $30 for one year (3 issues), $50 for two years (6 issues); $39 a year for institutions. Add $30 a year for international ($10 for Canada).

Upcoming: Winter 2012-13, a poetry and prose issue edited by John Skoyles and Ladette Randolph, will be published in December 2012. Spring 2013, a poetry and prose issue edited by Major Jackson, will be published in April 2013.

Submissions: Ploughshares has an updated reading period, as of June 1, 2010. The new reading period is from June 1 to January 15 (postmark and online dates). All submissions sent from January 16 to May 31 will be returned unread. Please see page 189 for editorial and submission policies, or visit our Web site: pshares.org/submit.

Back-issue, classroom-adoption, and bulk orders may be placed directly through *Ploughshares*. *Ploughshares* is also available as full-text products from EBSCO, H. W. Wilson, JSTOR, ProQuest, and the Gale Group. Indexed in M.L.A. Bibliography, Humanities International Index, Book Review Index. Full publishers' index is online at pshares.org. The views and opinions expressed in this journal are solely those of the authors. All rights for individual works revert to the authors upon publication. *Ploughshares* receives support from the National Endowment for the Arts and the Massachusetts Cultural Council.

Retail distribution by Ingram Periodicals, Media Solutions, and Ubiquity. Printed in the U.S.A. by The Sheridan Press.

Patricia Hampl photo by Barry Goldstein.

© 2012 by Emerson College   ISBN 978-1-933058-41-2
ISSN 0048-4474

CONTENTS
Fall 2012

INTRODUCTION
Patricia Hampl   7

NONFICTION
Charles Baxter, *What Happens in Hell*   13
Kelly Grey Carlisle, *A Goodly Heritage*   24
Robert Clark, *Snow on Snow*   36
Jennifer De Leon, *Mapping Yolanda*   39
Patricia Foster, *Inside*   49
Lynn Freed, *Gloria Mundi*   62
Mary Gordon, *The Taste of Almonds*   67
L. K. Hanson, *Some Pages from* The Story of My Hand   71
Phillip Lopate, *Why I Remain a Baseball Fan*   83
Nancy Lord, *My Acid Cruise*   90
David Stuart MacLean, *The Twittering Machine*   101
Thomas Mallon, *Forty More Years: Nixon and Me*   110
Kimberly Meyer, *What the Desert Said*   119
Eileen Pollack, *Didn't Anyone Tell You*   127
Ralph James Savarese, *Myself on High*   137
Dani Shapiro, *Evil Tongue*   141
Mark Slouka, *The Academy of Sciences*   151
Xu Xi, *My Mother's Story: The Fiction & Fact*   157

ABOUT PATRICIA HAMPL   168
A Profile by Jennifer Brice
REAL ESTATE   175
A Plan B Essay by Terese Svoboda
POSTSCRIPTS   177
Emerging Writer's Contest Winners
Dedications to Carl H. Klaus and David Hamilton
NOTES ON NEIHARDT   180
A Look2 Essay by Barry Gifford

EDITORS' SHELF	184
EDITORS' CORNER	184
CONTRIBUTORS' NOTES	185

Cover: L. K. Hanson, *Artistic Growth* (quotation from Willa Cather), 2010, pen, ink, color pencil, collage on paper, 8.5" x 6.5". Original (in slightly different form) appeared in the *Minneapolis Star Tribune,* January 2010. Courtesy of the artist, Minneapolis, Minnesota.

PLOUGHSHARES PATRONS

This nonprofit publication would not be possible without the support of our readers and the generosity of the following individuals and organizations.

CO-PUBLISHERS
Robert E. Courtemanche
The Green Angel Foundation
Marillyn Zacharis, in memory of Robert E. Courtemanche

COUNCIL
Jacqueline Liebergott

PATRONS
Eugenia Gladstone Vogel
Thomas E. Martin and Alice S. Hoffman
Dr. Jay A. Jackson and Dr. Mary Anne Jackson
Joanne Randall

FRIENDS
William H. Berman
Gregory Maguire
Elizabeth R. Rea of the Dungannon Foundation

ORGANIZATIONS
Emerson College
Massachusetts Cultural Council
National Endowment for the Arts

Co-Publisher: $10,000 for two lifetime subscriptions and acknowledgment in the journal for five years.

Council: $3,500 for two lifetime subscriptions and acknowledgment in the journal for three years.

Patron: $1,000 for a lifetime subscription and acknowledgment in the journal for two years.

Friend: $500 for acknowledgment in the journal for one year.

This all-essay issue of *Ploughshares*
is dedicated by Patricia Hampl to

Carl H. Klaus and David Hamilton
champions of the form

PATRICIA HAMPL
Introduction

When you visit the statue of Montaigne in Paris, you find him amidst overgrown greenery, almost sequestered in the bushes across from the Sorbonne, as if preferring, in bronze, the margin he chose in life. The first thing you notice is his shoe. Even at night, when I came upon him, the shoe emerges first, golden against the dusky bronze of his casually seated self, cross-legged, bending forward as if to catch what you might be saying there on the sidewalk.

People rub the shoe for luck or maybe out of affection. A shoe-rub is said to ensure a good exam result. It glows from all this human touch, an elegant sixteenth-century Mary Jane dancing slipper, blushing from generations of twentieth-century fondling. The sculptor, Paul Landowski, is better known for his gigantic 1931 Flash Gordon statue of Christ the Redeemer overlooking Rio de Janeiro. Montaigne's statue was done two years later, in 1933, perhaps to commemorate the four hundredth anniversary of his birth in 1533.

Something of the dandy about that shoe. Then you notice the face, surprisingly intent, looking back at you. The face of a man who appreciates the finer things, but is wryly amused by this weakness for pleasure, not haunted by his appetites. Landowski has given Montaigne a twentieth-century face, nonchalant, worldly, warm—almost an American face. A humanist face. This Montaigne, like the one I've been reading in recent years, sees it all and accepts it all in advance—the "all" of human perversity and contradiction played out on the field of avidity and longing.

It was raining that night, and though I'm urging a visit to the statue as if to a shrine, I didn't visit it. I just happened upon it, running late, trying to locate a fish restaurant recommended by a friend who knows Paris. Dripping in his leafy bower by the university, gleaming from the wet—or maybe because I'd been reading him, living with his sinuous sentences in my head, and had no idea such a statue existed—this bronze Montaigne had something of the apparition about him.

Like Whitman, another eccentric of the first person voice, he was loafing by the side of the road.

Out with the iPhone. Snap snap. Got the shoe. Didn't, couldn't quite, get the face. I had made an earlier pilgrimage to the famous tower on the chateau property near Bordeaux, had stood alone in the rounded room, imagined it once ringed with books, the stony enclosure where he devised his pieces, some shorter than a page, some long enough to make a chapbook, the writing he called his *essais*. He had refused to outfit this study with a fireplace (imagine the cold in winter) in order to safeguard his precious library.

I had checked out as well the adjacent alcove where he did allow a little fireplace, a cramped space to warm himself. On the walls I made out what was left of the painted frescoes (naked nymphs and godlets mostly, bundles of chipped floral decor) and the graffiti of earlier visitors—boldly scrawled *Emma 1882* and *Pierre 1920*, and someone whose name or message I couldn't decipher, the date 1989, the most recent I found.

I looked out the window of the alcove to experience (or think I was experiencing) his view. May, a great blossoming *marronnier,* part of an allée of chestnut trees marshaled along a gravel roadway leading to the tower. Nearer, just below, a triangular untended parterre garden where I imagined herbs (surely he ate well—he tells us he loved rich sauces, delicately flavored). I turned back toward the main room, his writing room, intending to take some descriptive notes, hoping for an insight for the book I was—I am—writing (an earnest essayist acting the part). With this in mind, turning quickly, gaze angled down to my notebook, I misjudged the space (an earlier century, a smaller scale) and smacked my head into the stone wall.

You do see stars. Or bits of white, spinning, that you could think of as stars.

Then, in my bell-ringing, star-shooting brain, I remembered that Montaigne had whacked his head too, colliding with another rider, knocked semiconscious from his horse as he rode his wooded property. He was taken for dead as his men carried him, insensible, back to the chateau. It is one of the few recognizably "memoiristic" vignettes in the *Essais,* a scrupulous reconstruction of this pivotal autobiographical episode, a bit of *story* in the midst of all his pages of musing, pondering, reflecting, wondering—what used to be called philosophizing.

Why did he honor this moment, so uncharacteristically, with narrative? Because, no doubt, it was a near-death experience. But even more, it was that most literary of experiences—unbiddable, decisive— the pivotal event that allowed him to pierce to the core of the creative imagination, perhaps for the first time. In being knocked off his horse, Montaigne experienced the doubleness necessary to empower personally voiced writing—maybe any writing. He experienced the fall—but he also *observed* the experience. Both, in separate but related strands of consciousness. The shock of this double register galvanized him to note the parallels of experience and observation. It was a kind of conversion moment. (No wonder that most notorious of conversions— St. Paul's—is often represented as a fall from his horse. Neither the fall nor the horse is mentioned in the Bible, but this is the standard image of his change of heart, as if the violence of being knocked down from a height were the only way to express it adequately. In a sense, Paul's fall is the spark moment of Christianity, a tumble from a smooth power ride, a thump out of self into a vision of a new world order.)

You get knocked off balance, off your assumptions. You see stars. Or what you take for stars. Your life changes, is changed. Even in our handy cliché, we routinely speak of being *struck* by this or that. The point is you *see*—a fresh kind of seeing that feels accurate because the self is not, for once, a subject you lug around, a slave to experience it must either simply endure or enjoy. It is revealed as an instrument you can use to render—if not "reality," then the experience of reality. The poetry of experience fastens to the reportage of the world.

To express accurately your experience you must, paradoxically, be knocked out of yourself—knocked out of the inevitable narcissism and egotism that is our narrative lot. This quicksilver experience has been given, by literature and psychology, the lackluster label *detachment*. Or as Keats called it—also fastening on an unwieldy phrase—*Negative Capability*. It is impossible to corral the experience in a name, a term, but once felt, there is nothing—not even love—to compare.

Montaigne's younger brother had been hit on the head too— a tennis ball to the temple. He didn't experience (so far as we know) detachment. He died of his blow (in the sixteenth century, tennis balls were made of wood). So perhaps Montaigne had an astonished, even slightly grateful/guilty sense of dumb luck in surviving his fall, because, unlike his brother, he "came to." But surely he registered as well—his description of the experience proves this—the significance of his head wound: it gave him a new, enlarged consciousness. In his *essais* he found the purpose of this self: to see and then to say.

The personal essay was born of that smack upside the head.

It is a cruel irony (is there any other kind?) that Montaigne's purposely evasive, even sassy, word for his writings—*essais*—has become that dread-dreary literary term, a word associated with Freshman English, the term paper, the school "theme." Is cigarette smoking harmful to your health? Discuss. Welcome back to school, children—describe your summer vacation. And just try to tell an agent or editor who has professed to admire your novel that you have "a book of essays" in the drawer. It has long been the genre that dares not speak its name in the literary marketplace.

Not Montaigne's fault. His book was an immediate bestseller. He thought he had decolonized writing, liberating it (or at least himself) from literary formality, to write freely—wild, untamed, eccentric, the last thing we think of when we hear the word "essay," that domesticated homework pet. He could just as easily have called his pieces his thingamajigs, and in fact his use of the word *essais* was meant to be just that, offhand, elusive, and undefined. *The New Yorker*'s old term for its front-of-the-book shorts—*casuals*—captures more what he had in mind in his attempt (that word! attempt, try, *essai*) to renew the springs of the first person voice bounding across the field of what we keep calling, against all the evidence, reality. But "reality" and individual experience are exactly what smack together (in the head, then on the page) in the essay. The personal and the public find perfect register—for the length of the thing, the length of the *essai,* the try.

Americans, in particular, love the first person voice. It's no coincidence that our greatest poem is "Song of Myself." We also seem to favor first person narrators for our classic novels—*Call me Ishmael... You don't know about me without you have read a book by the name of* The Adventures of Tom Sawyer; *but that ain't no matter... After Gatsby's death the East was haunted for me like that, distorted beyond my eyes' power of correction. So when the blue smoke of brittle leaves was in the air and the wind blew the wet laundry stiff on the line I decided to come back home...*

Or maybe we don't "love" the personal voice—we just trust it. It feels authentic to us, a people given the charge in our founding document to pursue happiness, always a singular enterprise. It may be our greatest fiction—to believe the personal voice is more "authentic" than other narrative modes. We'll take it, most of the time, over "omniscience." Not only because we are a notoriously self-regarding people, but because the first person voice opens the narrative door to speculation and reflection. Not to knowing, but to wondering. Perhaps we don't just want a story. We want the yakkety-yak of how it feels, how it seems. We want the story of thinking. How much of *Moby-Dick* is "story," and how much a vast tract, an ocean of essay, waves and swells of speculation attached to the adventure tale of the great white whale?

This is my letter to the world that never wrote to me—another poetic parent of the personal voice, speaking as usual in her sidelong way *(Tell the truth, but tell it slant)*.

Famously, rather coquettishly, Dickinson also said, *I'm Nobody! Who are you?* That apparent self-revelation (really a self-screening) and its waggish question display the economy shared by the personal voice in lyric poetry and the personal essay (two forms up to the same business). Of course you're nobody (so am I). But that fragile voice reveals more than a self. It holds the mirror up—not to itself but to the world. The essay is a solo dance, a private pirouette, its glowing footstep emerging onto the public street.

CHARLES BAXTER
What Happens in Hell

"Sir, I am wondering—have you considered lately what happens in Hell?"

No, I hadn't, but I liked that "lately." We were on our way from the San Francisco Airport to Palo Alto, and the driver for Bay Area Limo, a Pakistani American whose name was Niazi, was glancing repeatedly in the rearview mirror to check me out. After all, there I was, a privileged person—a hegemon of some sort—in the backseat of the Lincoln Town Car, cushioned by the camel-colored leather as I swigged my bottled water. Like other Americans of my class and station, I know the importance of staying hydrated. And there *he* was, up front, behind the wheel on a late sunny Saturday afternoon, speeding down California State Highway 101, missing (he had informed me almost as soon as I got into the car) the prayer service and sermon at his Bay Area mosque. The subject of the sermon would be Islamic inheritance laws—a subject that had led quite naturally to the subject of death and the afterlife.

I don't really enjoy sitting in the backseat of Lincoln Town Cars. I don't like being treated as some sort of important personage. I'm a Midwesterner by location and temperament and don't even cotton to being called "Sir." So I try to be polite ("Just call me Charlie") and take my shoes off, so to speak, in deference to foreign customs, as Mrs. Moore does in *A Passage to India*.

"No," I said, "I haven't. What happens in Hell?" I asked.

"Well," Niazi said, warming up and stroking his beard, "there is no forgiveness over there. There is forgiveness here but not there. The God does not listen to you on the other side."

"He doesn't?"

"No. The God does not care what you say, and He does not forgive you once you are on that side after you die. By then it is over."

"Interesting," I said, nondirectively.

"It is all in the Holy Book," Niazi went on. "And your skin, Sir. Do you know what the God does with your skin?"

"No, I don't," I said. "Tell me." Actually I was most interested in the definite article. Why was the deity referred to as *the* God? Are there still other lesser gods, minor subsidiary deities, set aside somewhere, who must be differentiated from the major god? I drank some more water as I considered this problem.

"It is very interesting, what happens with the skin," Niazi said, as we pulled off the Bayshore Freeway onto University Avenue. "Every day the skin is burned off."

"Yes?"

"Yes. This is known. And then, each day, the God gives you new skin. This new skin is like a sheath."

"Ah." I noticed the repeated use of the word *you*.

"And every day the *new* skin is burned off." He said this sentence with a certain degree of excitement. "It is very painful as you can imagine. And the pain is always *fresh* pain."

Meanwhile, we were proceeding through downtown Palo Alto. On the outskirts of town I had noticed the absence of pickup trucks and rusting American cars; everywhere I looked, I saw Priuses and Saabs and Lexuses and BMWs and Volvos and Mercedes-Benzes and a few Teslas here and there. The mix didn't include convertible Bentleys or Maybachs, the brand names that flash past you on Ocean Boulevard in Santa Monica. Here, ostentation was out; professional-managerial modesty was in. Here the drivers were engaged in Right Thinking and were uncommonly courteous: complete stops at stop signs were the norm, and ditto at the mere sight of a pedestrian at a crosswalk. No one seemed to be in a hurry. There was plenty of time for everything, as if Siddhartha himself were directing traffic.

And the pedestrians! Fit, smiling, upright, well-tended, with not a morbidly obese fellow-citizen in sight, the evening crowd on University Avenue appeared to be living in an earlier America era, one lacking desperation, hysteria, and Fox News. Somehow Palo Alto had remained immune to what one of my students has referred to as "The Great Decline." In this city, the businesses were thriving under blue skies and polished sunshine. I couldn't spot a single boarded-up front window. Although I saw plenty of panhandlers, no one looked shabby and lower-middle-class. I noted, as an outsider would, the lines outside the luxe restaurants—Bella Luna, Lavanda, and the others—everyone laughing and smiling. The happiness struck me as stagy. What phonies these people were! Having come from Minneapolis, where we have boarded-up businesses in bulk, I felt like—what is the expression?—an ape hanging onto the fence of Heaven watching the gods play.

And it occurred to me at that moment that Niazi felt that way too, apelike, except that I was one of those damn gods, which explained why he had to inform me about Hell.

"You burn forever," Niazi said, drawing me out of my reverie. "And, yes, here we are at your hotel."

"Sir" and "Hell": the two words belong together. After arguing with the hotel desk clerk, who claimed (until I showed him my confirmation number) that I didn't have a reservation and therefore didn't belong there, I went up to my room past a gaggle of beautiful leggy young men and women, track stars, in town for a meet at Stanford University, where I'd been hired to teach as a visiting writer. They were flirting with each other and tenderly comparing relay batons. Off in the bar on the other side of the lobby, drugstore cowboys were whooping it up, throwing back draft beers while the voice of Faith Hill warbled on the jukebox. Nothing is so dispiriting as the sight of strangers getting boisterously happy. It makes you feel like a stepchild, a poor relation. Having checked in, I went upstairs and sat in my room immobilized, unable for a moment even to open my suitcase, puzzled by the persistence of Hell and why I had just been forced to endure a lecture about it.

Rattled, I stared out the window. A soft Bay Area rain was falling, little dribs and drabs dropping harmlessly, impressionistically, out of the sky—Monet rain. A downmarket version of an Audubon bird—how I hate those Audubon birds—was trapped and framed in a picture above the TV.

I am usually an outsider everywhere. I don't mind being one—you're a writer, you choose a certain fate—but the condition is harder to bear in a self-confident city where everyone is playing a role successfully and no one is glancing furtively for the EXIT signs.

In his writings and his clinical practice, the French psychoanalyst

Jacques Lacan liked to ask why any particular person would *want* to believe any given set of ideas. He initially asked the question of behavioral psychologists with their dopey experiments with mice and pigeons, but, inspired by Lacan, you can ask it of anyone. Why do you *desire* to believe the ideas that you hold dear, the cornerstones of your faith? Why do you clutch tightly to the ideas that appear to be particularly repellant and cruel? Why would anyone *want* to suppose that an untold multitude of human souls burn in extreme agony for eternity? Having left a marriage, and now living and working alone, I found myself in that hotel room experiencing the peculiar vacuum of self that arises when you go on working without a clear belief in what (or whom) you're working *for* and are also being exposed randomly to the world's cruelties.

The idea of Hell has a transcendently stupefying ugliness akin to that of torture chambers. This particular ugliness is fueled by the rage and sadism of the believer who enjoys imagining his enemies writhing perpetually down there in the colorful fiery pit. How many of us relish the fairy tale of endless suffering! Nietzsche claimed that all such relishers are in the grip of *ressentiment*, whereby frustration against the rulers, and anger at oneself, are transformed into a morality. Ressentiment is what happens to resentment once it goes Continental and becomes a metaphysical category. After Marx, injustice no longer seemed part of a natural order. And if injustice *isn't* part of a natural order, then ressentiment will naturally arise, the rage of the have-nots against the haves, the losers against the winners. Sometimes the rage is constructive, sometimes not. For Nietzsche, in *On the Genealogy of Morals,* the unequal distribution of power is simply a condition of things-as-they-are:

> *It is not surprising that the lambs should bear a grudge against the great birds of prey, but that is no reason for blaming the great birds of prey for taking the little lambs. And when the lambs say among themselves, "These birds of prey are evil, and he who least resembles a bird of prey, who is rather its opposite, a lamb,—should he not be good?"*

If you're a loser, you might as well get used to your loserdom and sanctify it. Thus Nietzsche. The eagles will come down sooner or later and grab you and eat you. It's how nature works. But if you, the lamb, claim a superior virtue to the eagle, and you band together with other lambs and consign the eagles to a sadistically picturesque Hell, you will, in another life, find yourself behind the wheel, working for Bay Area Limo, instructing the hapless pale-skinned passenger from Minnesota about the manner in which some will find themselves scorched forever on the other side, forever and forever, oh, and by the way, here we are at your hotel.

In one of Alice Munro's stories, a character observes that the Irish treat all authority with abject servility followed by savage, sneering mockery. Ressentiment has its comic side, after all.

After washing up, I came back downstairs through the lobby—more beautiful track stars, more flirting, and a little micro-portion of ressentiment on my part against their beauty and youth and sexiness—and ambled to the Poolside Grille, where I ordered the *specialité de la maison,* blackened red snapper (California cuisine: black beans, jasmine rice, salsa fresca, lime sour cream), the snapper itself an endangered species. I hastily gulped down my chardonnay and, like a starving peasant, devoured the fish without tasting it. Gulping and chewing and swallowing, I watched the athletes in their skimpy garb promenading around the hotel, as graceful as swans. Ned Rorem on youth: "We admire them for their beauty, and they want us to admire them for their minds, the little shits." All the while Niazi's voice was in my head: "Every day the God gives you a new skin so that He can burn it away." I paid the bill and returned to my room. Fresh pain! What a phrase. I couldn't read, so I watched TV: *CSI: Crime Scene Investigation,* Captain Jim Brass confessing to human failings, played very well by Paul Guilfoyle. Or did I watch another show, some prepackaged drama interchangeable with that one? I can't remember. I do remember that I drifted off to sleep in my street clothes. There was no one around to tell me not to.

I didn't see Niazi again for another four weeks. On a Wednesday morning in April, he was to meet me in front of my Stanford apartment at 9:30 to take me to the San Francisco Airport so that I could fly back to Minneapolis. I had been commuting almost every week. At 9:25 I stood out in front with my suitcase beside me, waiting for him. I saw his black Lincoln Town Car in the visitors' parking lot. He honked, pulled up, and rushed out to put my suitcase in the trunk.

"Good morning, Sir," he said. "How are you?" His eyes, I noticed, were heavy-lidded and puffy. He looked like a box turtle.

"Fine," I said, settling into the backseat and snapping on the lap-and-shoulder belt. "How about you?" I looked around for a bottle of water. There were two little ones.

"Very tired," he said, checking his watch before flopping in behind the wheel. "I could not sleep last night. I have been in this parking lot since 8:30."

"You should have called me," I said. "We could've left early."

"No no no," Niazi corrected me. "I have been trying to take the nap."

"Are you still drowsy?" I asked, noting again his nonstandard use of definite articles.

"A little, somewhat," he told me. "But when I am that way, I think of the Holy Book."

"Ah."

He drove us up to Interstate 280, back in the hills, an alternative route to the airport. Here the rain was falling harder, and I noticed that Niazi didn't bother to turn on the car's windshield wipers. The rain spattered violently against the glass in an almost Midwestern manner. I felt right at home. Stroking his beard, Niazi gazed out at the highway, and after about ten minutes, I saw that, with his eyes half-closed, he was moving his head back and forth, shaking it slowly, as if... *was this possible? Was I actually seeing what I was seeing?* He was driving the limo, with me in it, while sleeping.

My brother Tom used to get drowsy behind the wheel and, one winter night in 1961, almost killed himself outside Delano, Minnesota, when he dozed off. Another irony: Delano's major business in those days was the engraving of cemetery monuments, and the town's motto was, "Drive carefully. We can wait." Unable to walk away from his accident, his car in the ditch, my brother had to drag himself on all fours out of the wreck across a snowy field to a farmhouse. As a boy, I was quite accustomed to my brother's sleepiness behind the wheel and would keep him entertained and awake with bright patter, for which I have a gift. So: "Niazi!" I said. "Do you have many jobs today? I'll bet you do!"

"Oh, yes, Sir," he said dispiritedly. "Many. Two this afternoon." Maybe he wasn't asleep after all.

The rain fell harder, unusually hard for Northern California. I looked around at the interior of the Lincoln Town Car, thinking, *We're going to crash. But at least this limo is a very solid car.* With the irony of which life is so fond, I thought of two lines of a creepy song I had heard a few months before, by the group Concrete Blonde. The song was "Tomorrow, Wendy," and two lines serve as the song's refrain:

> *Hey, hey, goodbye*
> *Tomorrow Wendy's going to die.*

And just about then the car began to fishtail. When a car fishtails, you take your foot off the accelerator and tap the brake pedal. Fishtailing occurs often in icy conditions (think: Minnesota winter), less often in rain. But California drivers aren't used to precipitation, so when the car began to lose control, Niazi woke up and slammed on the brakes, throwing the Lincoln into a sideways skid, and when the rear-wheel-drive tires acquired traction again, they pushed us off the freeway, onto the shoulder, and then, very rapidly, down a hill, where the car flipped over sideways and began to roll, turning over and over and over, until it reached the bottom of the hill, right side up. From the moment the car began to lose control until it came to rest, Niazi was screaming. All during the time we turned over down that hill, he continued to scream.

Reader, this essay is about that scream. Please do your best to imagine it.

Men don't scream, as a rule; they bellow or roar with fright or anger, but male screaming is an exceptionally rare phenomenon, and the sound makes your flesh crawl. A woman's scream calls you to protective action. A man's scream provokes horror.

Inside that car, I was holding on to the door's hand rest, clutching it, and I was as quiet as the tomb. I wasn't particularly scared, although things were flying around the car—my cell phone had escaped from my coat pocket and was airborne in front of me, as were various other items from the car, including those free little bottles of water and a clipboard from the front seat—and I heard the sound of crunching or of some huge animal chewing up the car. I thought: *Let this be over soon.* And then it was. They say everything slows down during an accident, but no, not always, and this accident didn't slow down my sense of time until we were at rest and I heard Niazi moaning, and more than anything else I wanted to get out of that car before the gas tank exploded, but my door wouldn't open—the right rear door—but the left rear door did, after I pushed my shoulder against it.

Around and inside the car was a terrible smell of wreckage, oil and burnt rubber, and another smell, which I am tempted to describe as sulfurous.

"Niazi," I said, "are you OK?"

"Oh oh oh oh," he said, "yes, I am OK" (he clearly wasn't), "and you, Mr. Baxter, sir, are you OK?"

"Yes." Where was I? Without a transition, I seemed to be standing in the rain outside the car, and Niazi, making the sounds that precede speech in human history, was trying to get himself off the ground, blood streaming down his face; and his shoes, I noticed, were off, which (I had once heard) is one of the signs of a high-velocity accident. Amid the wreckage, he was barefoot, and blood was dripping onto his feet. I reached out for him.

Suddenly witnesses surrounded us. "You turned over four times!" an Asian American man said, clutching my arm. His face was transfixed by shock. "I saw it. I was behind you. Are you all right? How could you possibly be all right? Surely you are not all right?" He opened his umbrella and lifted it over my head, a perfect gesture of kindness.

"I don't know," I said. I looked down at my Levis. The belt loops had snapped off. How was that possible? I stared in wonderment at the broken belt loops. I looked at the man. "Am I all right?"

He simply stared at me as if I had been resurrected.

The usual confusion followed: EMT guys, California Highway Patrol guys, witness reports. An off-duty cop from San Marino, another witness to the accident, said he couldn't believe I was standing up. He touched my arm with a tender gesture as if I might break. Someone asked me to sign a document, and I did, my hand shaking so violently that my signature looked like that of a third grader. And what was I worried about? My *laptop*. Had it been damaged? Furthermore, I thought, I'm going to be late for my airplane flight! In shock, we lose all sense of proportion. My signature on another official document looked like someone else's, not mine. And now Niazi was standing up, still bloodily barefoot, talking. He appeared to be in stable condition though they were putting a head brace on him and then lowering him onto a wooden stretcher, as if he had been smashed up. The Asian American witness who saw our car turn over four times asked me where I was going, and I said, "To the airport."

"I will take you," he said. "Just put your suitcase in the backseat. We will have to drop off my father-in-law in Millbrae. Do you mind?"

"No," I said. "Thank you."

The driver and his father-in-law spoke Mandarin all the way to Millbrae, the driver politely interpreting for me so that I wouldn't be left out of the conversation. "My father-in-law thinks you must be badly injured," the driver said. "I told him that you said you were fine." Thanks to this gentleman, I arrived at the San Francisco Airport in time for my flight. My ribs hurt, and my back hurt, and I gave off an odd panic-stricken body odor, but all I wanted to do was to get home. At the same time, I was still disoriented. Near the entrance to Terminal One, I noticed, was a sign with a name on it: NOSMO KING. It appeared to me as graffiti on behalf of a deposed potentate. Who was this oddly named Nosmo King? King of what? We were in Northern California! No kings here! Not until I was seated on the airplane did I calm down and realize that I had misread the sign and that, like other public places, the San Francisco Airport did not tolerate lighting up or puffing on cigarettes.

*

My back still hurts sometimes, especially on long flights. Niazi called me at home a few days later and left a message on my answering machine. His voice was expressive of deep despair combined with physical pain. "Mr. Baxter, sir, I am worried about you. I am...I am not all right, but I am lying down, recovering. Would you please call me?"

No. I would not call him, and I did not. I still haven't. I heard from someone else that he had broken his back. Guiltily, shamefully, I left him uncalled, and my inability to dial his number and to ask him how he was recovering surely serves as a sign of a human failing, a personalized grudge that will not be appeased. But all I could think of then and now was: *that expert on Hell almost got me killed.*

The insurance company has promised to send me $500 to compensate me for my pain and suffering.

In another version of the accident, the one I sometimes told myself compulsively, I sit silently while Niazi screams and the car rolls over down the hill. But I didn't just tell myself this story; I told everybody. The accident turned me into a tiresome raconteur. A repetition compulsion had me in its tight narrative grip. I had become like a character in one of my own stories, the sort of madcap who buttonholes an innocent bystander to relieve himself of an obsession. Some stories present themselves as a gift, to be handed on to others as a second gift. But some more dire stories have a certain difficult-to-define taint. They give off an odd smell. They have infected the person who possesses them, and that person peevishly passes on the infection to others. In the story in which I am the victim, I am not an artist, but a garrulous ancient mariner who has come ashore long after his boat has been set adrift and long after his rescue, which does not feel like a rescue but an abandonment.

From the airport I called my wife, from whom I was—and remain—separated, to give her the news. She met me at the airport, and we hugged each other for the first time in months. Near-death trumps marital discord but does not heal it. Then she took me back to my apartment, where she dropped me off.

I sat alone in the apartment for a few days, trying to read, but mostly writing e-mails. At night, I would fall asleep to the remembered sound of Niazi's screams. I announced my accident on Facebook, curious whether any of my FB friends would press the "like" button. A few did. I picked up the phone and started calling people. "Let me tell you what happened to me," I would say. I had become strangely interesting to myself. One friend has called my compulsion to talk about the accident a form of "vocational imperialism," though I think he means *avocational* imperialism. After all, I am a mere tourist in the landscape of Islam. As an unsteady humanist, I don't believe in much, and the virtues that I do believe in—goodness, charity, bravery—abandoned me in the moments after that accident.

All I thought as we tumbled down that hill, as I have said, was the hope that this awfulness would be over soon. We die alone, even if someone else is dying beside us. And—this was my fleeting wish in the backseat of that violently rotating Lincoln Town Car, in the wondrously dark clarity of thought produced by the unexpected, as the plastic bottles of water were flying around my head and my cell phone twirled in the air in front of me—I prayed that the car would land right-side up or, if this was to be the moment of my death, by fire as the gas tank exploded, that it be quick.

KELLY GREY CARLISLE
A Goodly Heritage

> "This structure has two helical chains each coiled around the same axis... It has not escaped our notice that the specific pairings we have postulated immediately suggest a possible copying mechanism for the genetic material."
> —J. D. Watson and Francis Crick, on their discovery of the structure of DNA.

I.

In 1972, my father-in-law, Ron, built a table of cherry wood, gave it a hand-rubbed finish, and presented it to his wife, Susan. Thirty-five years later, its surface is scratched with a hundred fine marks. The varnish has worn off around its edges and the exposed wood glows where his children slouched as they did their homework or leaned to reach the salt or pass the bread. Its finish is dulled in circles where Christmas cookies were set to cool every year for thirty years. The table is beautiful, in spite of—or because of—the worn edges, the dull cookie spots, the scratches. But tonight Susan notices a new, deep scratch, and my husband, Ben, and I watch her fill it in carefully with brown polish. Once she's done, she waxes the table top and buffs it to a shine, then steps back to look. It's two in the morning on New Year's Day. We've all been thinking the same thing since midnight: this is the first year Susan will spend without her husband, the first year her children will spend without their father.

Everywhere in this house, there are reminders of Ron. Scrolls of Japanese calligraphy on the walls, a navy kimono at the top of the stairs. Ron loved all things Japanese and practiced Buddhist meditation. He loved music, and his Möller pipe organ, viols, and shakuhatchi take up a room in the basement. We knew which hymns to pick for his funeral; his favorites were marked with fingerings. There are beautiful objects everywhere in this house—eighteenth-century Japanese textiles, nineteenth-century blue willow plates, a Buddhist heart sutra carved into wood. Treasures aside, the house is modest, built in the 1970s in what was then a new suburb north of Atlanta. What was once a shiny, new starter home is no longer shiny or new. The floor buckles in the hall; the bedroom carpet is the same moss green Ben crawled across as a baby; the deck is rotting away. Ron and Susan had enough money to move to a luxury home in a fancy new development. Instead, they made do with the house and bought art, handmade things from all over the world, and books. Lots of books.

Of all the beautiful objects Ron left to his family, the most treasured are the pieces of furniture he built: table, silver chest, and dictionary stand, the chest of drawers, the nightstand, the master bed. His wife—his widow—is surrounded by the work of his hands: wood chosen with care, cut and shaped, sanded and polished until it glowed.

In the few weeks since he died, it has become a family game to find Ron in his children. "Oh!" we say when Ben or his sister does something especially Ron-like, "I know where you got that gene!" For some reason it's easier to name these similarities now that he is dead—the free-roaming intellect, the love of music and ice cream, the formidable independence, and its corollary, an infuriating stubbornness. I'm amazed to look at a child and see the parent—to know where the smile, the eyes, the laugh, the stubbornness, the music originated.

No one will ever tell me that I look like my father.

II.

We inherit our genes from our parents, as our parents did from theirs, and therefore DNA isn't just the blueprint for your body—your straight or curly hair, your asthma, or intelligence—it's your history too. Your DNA can trace the story of your ancestors, who they were and where they came from and with whom they mated, the patterns of their migrations, all the way back through the generations to the very beginning of humankind.

You might think of DNA as a history book, something like *The Story of Civilization,* only even longer, and all about you. According to the

Human Genome Project, the initiative that sequenced human DNA, if your genetic code were printed in such a book, it would be over three billion letters long. The book would be bound in two hundred volumes, each a thousand pages long. The text of the history book would read something like this—ATGCTCGAAGA—200,000 pages of it, single-spaced, in agate type. A, T, C, and G are the four letters that constitute the alphabet of the genome. They're not really letters, but the four nucleotides of DNA: adenine, guanine, thymine, cytosine. Different combinations of these four chemicals provide both the directions for making your body and clues about where you come from.

We're just learning to read the coded language this history is written in, for it is ancient and complex. DNA is a timeless tongue, older than we are, formulated long before humans knew how to read, before we knew how to make fire, maybe even before we knew how to love.

Sometimes I think that when God said, "Let the earth bring forth the living creature after his kind," and when he said, "Let us make man in our image," what slipped from his mouth were not words as we understand them but, instead, that ancient, inscrutable language. Adenine, cytosine, guanine, thymine, swirled together in their double-helix, slipping like a silver chain from His mouth to the earth into the cells of whatever primal form evolved into us.

It isn't difficult to isolate DNA, as I learned in college biology. You can do it at home with some spinach, a blender, dish soap, meat tenderizer, and rubbing alcohol. Pure DNA is translucent, sometimes milky white, sometimes crystal clear. It falls slowly, like liquid glass from a stirring rod. I'm always amazed that something so important, so thick with vital information, should be almost transparent. There, lying cool in the palm of your hand, the physical heritage of all living things. It's as simple as that—take hold of your inheritance.

III.

It's 1976 and three weeks after she gives birth to me, my mother, Michele, leaves me with some friends in a motel room they share near Sunset Boulevard, in Hollywood, California. Her beaten and strangled body is found the next morning.

At first, I live with my maternal grandmother, who is not married to my grandfather. She dies when I am four years old. I am then sent to live with my grandfather Richard and his wife, Marilyn, who raise me.

I'll never know my genetic father.

I inherit one of my mother's possessions, a Bible she had as a child. I lose it when I leave for college. I inherit my grandmother's camera and some of her jewelry. I'll never use them.

My mother's murder remains unsolved.

When I'm twenty-eight, I call the LAPD to check on her case. I am the first person to have called in twenty years. The cold-case detective tells me that they might have a chance to solve it if they can find usable DNA on the physical evidence stored in her file. They don't find any DNA.

IV.

A few days after his father, Ron, dies, my husband, Ben, tells me that if there is a heaven, the idea doesn't really make him feel better.

We're driving along I-75, and even at seventy miles per hour, cars still pass us, right and left, racing each other to the next bend in the road. This is Atlanta after all, where the slow time of the South speeds up to something frantic, panicked.

"I can't imagine my father up there on his own," Ben says. "His family was the most important thing to him. How can heaven be heaven without your family?"

I tell him what my friend Carol says, that time in heaven is different from time on earth. We on earth see a separation—Ron was with us, and now he isn't. But the separation doesn't occur in heaven. Ron is there now, but so also are we. In fact, all of us on earth have also been in heaven since the beginning of time. We are there now, with all of those who came before us and all of those who will come after us, all those whom we love and all those whom we never knew, our ancestors and descendants from all time. Everything occurring in the present.

I can't tell if this makes him feel better.

V.

Blood is important, my grandfather tells me. It's who you are.

I'm a little girl when he tells me this.

His fat belly presses against the table, his undershirt rides up to his navel. He doesn't see very well, and when he doesn't have his contacts in, his thick glasses look like the bottoms of beer bottles. It's hard to tell what he is thinking when he wears his glasses, because you can't see his eyes. You can't tell if he's looking down at the table or over your shoulder, but you can always tell when he wants you to believe what he's saying. He takes off his thick glasses and looks straight at you with his blind eyes.

My grandfather takes off his glasses when he tells me the story of our family.

He tells me how my grandmother, the one I used to live with, was half Native Hawaiian. He tells me how her father was full-blooded Hawaiian, and a cliff diver, and how this explains why I like to swim and why I turn so dark in the sun.

My grandfather, who is English, tells me how he himself is related to the Earl Grey of tea fame and Lady Jane Grey of beheading fame, and how, somewhere in England, our family has a house named Fallodon. This is important, he tells me, because it means we have noble blood.

On some nights, my grandfather tells me the story of his own childhood, how he, too, was an orphan. How his parents were killed by the Spanish Flu, how he was raised by many different people, how he went to Cambridge, how he was drafted into the Navy.

On the nights we watch old movies together, ones like *Sherlock Holmes: Terror by Night* and *Hobson's Choice,* he tells me how he used to work in film. How, after he moved to America, he wrote scripts for *Perry Mason* and *The Twilight Zone.* How he was the cousin of the English actor Robert Donat and how he'd known Lawrence Olivier, Ava Gardner, Claire Bloom, and John Wayne.

Sometimes, he tells me he was also a chef at the Savoy, a secret agent, a movie director, a knight, a baronet, a race car driver, a chorister, a bum.

Some nights, after we've gone to bed, my grandfather screams in his sleep. He wakes us all with his cries. In the morning, he tells me not to worry—he was just dreaming about the War. He tells me how he served in the Navy on Mountbatten's ship, how he went to India, how he was at Dunkirk, how he was recruited for Secret Operations, how he was caught behind enemy lines committing sabotage. He was tortured and starved, and this is why he panics in crowds, why he won't wait in lines at restaurants, why he eats whole meals in the middle of the night. That this is why he screams in his sleep.

All these things are important to know, my grandfather tells me, because where you come from is important to know. He tells me that of my English, Hawaiian, and blue blood, the most important is the English blood. The blood of Shakespeare and Nelson and Churchill run in my veins and I must never forget this. On some nights, he tells me I'm half English, because he forgets that I'm not really his daughter; he forgets that my mother, his murdered daughter, ever came between us.

And then, once he's finished telling me stories, he puts his glasses back on, his eyes once more obscured.

By the time my grandfather dies, when I am twenty-one, I have stopped believing everything he ever said.

VI.

You can find out a lot about your ancestry on the Internet, if you know where to look.

My great-grandfather—the Native Hawaiian cliff diver—was actually a half-Hawaiian casting director and movie extra in the 1930s and '40s. If you print out the appropriate form and include a money order for $10, the State of Hawaii will send you a copy of your ancestor's birth certificate. After eight months, the State of Hawaii writes to tell me that my great-grandfather does not exist. And they're keeping my $10.

The Internet says my grandfather did write for *Perry Mason*. He wrote a whole six episodes out of 271. Fallodon, our supposed ancestral manor, really is the seat of the Earls Grey—though the Internet also says that there are many families of Greys, most of whom are not earls.

My grandfather said he'd served in the Royal Navy before he became a spy and was captured by the Nazis, but he had no medals, no discharge certificate, no photographs. And yet he knew the name for every esoteric part of a ship, could tie knots, even with weak eyes and arthritic fingers. When I was eight years old, he bought a boat; when I was in sixth grade, we moved on board to live. The Royal Navy's Web site says that it will send you the service file for a deceased serviceman if you can provide proof of his death, permission from his next of kin, and a check drawn in pounds sterling. The check must say "Sterling" on the front, or they can't take it, and that is more difficult to find than you might think. But finally, I mail everything to England and wait.

Two months later, the Royal Navy writes to tell me, very politely, that they've never heard of my grandfather. They don't mention the pounds sterling.

VII.

After searching for twenty minutes, I finally locate Disc 3313 at the library. It's crammed among the other vinyl records on a dusty metal shelf in the corner of a media room where shiny flat screen monitors and DVDs are beginning to crowd out the shelves of microfiche. The cardboard album feels awkward after years of holding CDs in their efficient cases. When I get to the counter, I ask the work-study student if I can check out the record. She supposes so, but says she'll have to ask to be sure.

"It's not like we have anything to play it on here," she says.

But after typing for a few minutes and making several phone calls, she says that no one at the library knows how to check out a record. When they switched everything from stamped cards to bar codes, they forgot the LPs. No one knows how to check anything out without a bar code.

Another twenty minutes later, cradling the newly bar-coded record as I walk to the car, I notice that it hasn't been checked out since 1970, six years before I was born.

*

Once I learn how to read, my grandfather starts taking me to the bookstore with him. I wander the aisles freely while he peruses the latest in biography and spy fiction. He buys us each one book, and I can pick any book I want because he never looks at the covers before he pays. If I stay in the kids' section where I belong, I pick out Richard Scarry books, Dr. Seuss, Caldecott Medal winners. When I explore the rest of the store, sometimes my choices don't work out as well, titles like *100 Coupons for Romance* (which I pick when I'm six because of the cupids and the hearts on the cover) or the abridged *Journals of Lewis and Clark* (which I pick a few years later for the sketches of fish inside).

One day when I'm eight or nine, I pick a cassette of the Old Vic's recording of T. S. Eliot's play, *Murder in the Cathedral*. I choose it for its promising black cover that has a stained glass window and a shiny sword dripping with blood. I think it'll be a mystery, like the Sherlock Holmes stories I've been reading, but it isn't. Eliot's verse play about the twelfth-century martyrdom of Thomas Becket, Archbishop of Canterbury, is disappointing when I can't understand the plot. But unlike my other unhappy purchases, I don't set the tape aside or lose it. I listen to it over and over and over again. I listen to it as I go to sleep, night after night, because I like the way the words sound, the elegant cadences of the English actors, the chant of the monks, the mournful chorus of women. Listening to their voices in the dark, I imagine myself in that big church far away in England, imagine that my nightlight is the flicker of candles on stone walls. I feel safe in that place of my imagining, content, at home.

When I listen to the recording in my thirties—for the first time as an adult—a record borrowed from the library spinning on my husband's turntable, the sun just setting, the scent of our dinner still hanging in the air, I wonder how on earth I should have found that play comforting, how I should have thought of Canterbury, where murder was committed, as a peaceful place.

Or, perhaps, listening to the library's record, I don't wonder but *know,* because by then I am a Christian, a member of the Episcopal church, a branch of the Anglican communion, the church Henry VIII founded when he broke with Rome. Canterbury Cathedral is the home of the Anglican Church. By then, I am also a grad student in English.

When I listen to that record as an adult, I recognize in Eliot's verse the cadence of my prayer book, the heritage of a thousand years of English poetry.

What *does* make me wonder, though, is this: when I finally pull the record from the library shelf, I notice a familiar face on its cover. My grandfather's supposed cousin, the actor Robert Donat, there, in the starring role.

VIII.

Twenty-two years after I first dreamt of Canterbury Cathedral, my husband, his mother, and I stand at the place where Thomas Becket was martyred. It is the summer before Ron dies. He decided not to come with us, having already been to England. The three of us are on tour with a church choir, spending a week in residence at Westminster Abbey in London. This is our free day. Canterbury is the place Chaucer's pilgrims were headed, just a few of the thousands who traveled each year to visit Becket's shrine. In a way, we're pilgrims too.

I find it sad sometimes that my branch of Christianity has lost the old obsession with pilgrimage, relics, and shrines. Martyrs and saints—the company of believers, known and unknown—are our spiritual ancestors, though we may have no genetic or even cultural connection. "The Lord is the portion of my inheritance," says the Psalmist, "yea, I have a goodly heritage." The *Book of Common Prayer* puts it another way: "Your heritage is the faith of patriarchs, prophets, apostles, and martyrs, and those of every generation who have looked to God in hope."

To visit the place where someone has died, or was born, or worked, or was buried—to touch it, even—is the closest physical connection the living can make with the dead. For this reason, we leave stones on graves, finger names on a black stone wall, touch a worn table made of cherry wood. The stone floor by Becket's shrine bears twin indentations, worn there over the years by pilgrim knees.

Ben, Susan, and I stand in the north transept of the cathedral, just off the cloisters, in a small stone room with high ceilings, connected to the nave by a wide stone staircase. Thomas was killed at the bottom of the stairs. It was evening. He'd been saying Vespers with his monks when Henry's knights burst in. They pulled Thomas to the stairs, but he would not leave the sanctuary, so they killed him where he stood. He offered no resistance, only a prayer. I imagine the awful silence that followed the knights' departure, the quiet moment between the slamming of the door and the monks' screams. The priest crumpled on the stairs. I imagine the blood flowing, meandering in the channels between these gray stones, pooling, flowing softly, without sound.

Eight hundred years later, if I knelt at the stairs and touched my hand to the place he died, might there still be microscopic traces of blood, bits of DNA trapped in the pores of stone? If I touched my hand to the place he died, would I be touching him?

IX.

The day after we go to Canterbury, that summer before Ron dies, I lie in the organ loft of Westminster Abbey while our friend David practices for Sunday's service. It's seven-thirty in the evening, long after all the tourists have left. The great church is empty—the marshals in their red gowns, the vergers and clergy in their black cassocks have all gone home. David, Ben, Susan, and I are the only four people in a church that on an average day sees three thousand visitors. The summer light still filters through the stained glass windows, a slant light slowly fading—what is called the vesper light.

Earlier in the day, I visited the Family History Center to request my grandfather's birth certificate and the birth, death, and marriage certificates of his parents. When I get back home to the States, I'll use those certificates to trace his family back five generations—not, as he claimed, to earls and queens, but to electrical engineers, shopkeepers, and millwrights in Northumberland. Never will I have been prouder of my heritage.

I lie flat on my back in the organ loft, gazing at the vaulted ceiling. Directly beneath me is the memorial to Newton, and to its right, the tomb of Charles Darwin. Here, buried or memorialized, are the "great and the good" of this land, the heritage of a nation. To my right, in the east end of the church, kings and queens: the sainted Edward the Confessor, Elizabeth I, Henry V, on and on. In the Poets Corner: Keats, Blake, Chaucer, Eliot. Scattered throughout the church, my husband's beloved Howells, Stanford, Purcell, Handel. Although we were not born here, English is our language too, and it is easy to feel as if these great and good are our heritage as well.

Here, now, gazing at the ceiling above, the power of this place, a power beyond the great weight of stone, comes streaming down—the power of time, of history. A history that resides not in the tombs and memorials of famous men, but in the hundreds of thousands of pilgrims who have wandered these aisles, the thousands who still come today. Every tourist here is a pilgrim. They may not come seeking Christ or a saint, but they still *seek*. A student, all glasses and untamed hair and wrinkled shirt, looking for the tomb of her favorite poet, a scientist finding Darwin or Newton or Kelvin, a German woman looking for Diana—she isn't buried here—they're all seeking something. The power of this place comes not from memorials or tombs, but from the susurration of a million prayers made to God and Christ and Lady and Saint—the whispered thoughts to Darwin, Newton, Chaucer, Diana—these have consecrated this place, more deeply than any holy oil or water.

In my mind's eye, I see the whole church, the quire and altar at its center. I imagine all those who've walked here before me, from all ages, all here at once, something like a time-lapse photograph. There they all are, thousands on thousands of them, in shorts and jeans, hoop skirts and top hats, gowns and doublets. They swirl around the church like the pilgrims at Mecca, a sea of humans come to touch the black stone of the Kaaba, to kiss what Mohammed himself kissed.

My own faith, just one among many, teaches that all humans are related, that we are family. The story goes like this: we are all descended from one man, Adam, and all redeemed by one Man, making us the sons and daughters of God. All human beings are His children, and therefore, all human beings are brothers and sisters.

Science teaches that we are all related too. Our mitochondrial DNA shows that, more or less directly, we come from the same place—even perhaps the same mother—in Africa. We share the same ancient parents, the same biological heritage. Somewhere beneath me, as I lie here in the organ loft, is the man who made our knowledge of this possible, who first traced patterns of descent through the ages, the ancestry and heritage of all creation. And why, I wonder, are we told we must believe in Evolution *or* Religion, when they teach us the same thing: that every man is a brother, a father, a son to us; every woman a sister, a mother, a daughter.

I lie on my back in Westminster Abbey, above the tombs of Newton and Darwin, and stare at the vaulted ceiling. There is a motif painted along the edge of each arch. It is a delicate chain; a rose sits within each circular link. A chain, symbol of connection; the rose, symbol of Mary, source of Christ's humanity, his biology. The chain, the bond that connects every human. The chain that links all of us who live to those who came before to those who will come after, stretching unbroken from the beginning to the end of time. In the vesper light, it twirls like the double helix.

ROBERT CLARK
Snow on Snow

Snow had fallen, snow on snow,
Snow on snow,
In the bleak mid-winter
Long ago.

You probably know these lines, either from Christina Rossetti's poem of 1871 or, more likely, Holst's setting of them as a carol. I used one of them as the title of a book, "bleak" altered to "deep" by the publisher, who thought "bleak" too bleak.

Which it might indeed be. Rossetti was melancholic, iced up with unversed emotion, with passions gone gelid that, reticent and gob-stopped, couldn't quite state their names. She was a devout Anglo-Catholic. Her worship at Christ Church in London's Camden Town fumed with incense and candles, ardent for the Eucharist. Ever virgin, dazzled and expectant, she posed for Annunciations by her brother Gabriel and his Pre-Raphaelite cohort.

Critics say her prosody had its roots in nursery rhymes, the tick-tock of fortunes and unravelings, of goblins vanquished, of witches made meek, of children saved and of children saving all—of things coming round upon themselves. Still, I say it was snow. She might have been cold, and then again she must have been misunderstood. Isn't that what children always and everywhere are—misunderstood?

When I see snow falling, I hear a clock ticking; the clock next to the bed upon which my mother holds me, her heart its counterpoint; and the snow unwinds, sheathes and coils like drapery, like the shade that, as she leaves, cascades down the window sash. The clock gets lost in my own heartbeat and outside—you know this; you hear it ticking, swinging on its pendulum—the snow falls and will fall for as long as it takes to cover everything. A car will drive by, headlights tunneling, the tires a whir and then a rustle compressed to a sigh. There is a great clockwork above you in heaven, geared and laboring, and it will spin all night until there is nothing but snow. It will do the work. You may rest. Angels will watch over your bed. They descend upon you like snow. Like a bell in the night, it tolls until it's put the world to sleep, rung it into silence.

I will wake in the morning and it will be like Christmas: I will race to see what great thing has been accomplished, what thing—vouchsafed in the night—I've been given. And what I have is a world erased, whited out, veiled and muffled; snow on snow and then, for good measure (as Rossetti has it in the poem), snow on snow again. There's no time, only space. I am sub specie aeternitatis. There will be no more suffering. It has been laid down and covered over, swaddled in boundless white. Peace: that's how it is for me, swaddled too. I have the snow to keep me warm.

Rossetti did not see it this way. In another poem, she finds a bird dead of cold and says, "Dig him a grave where the soft mosses grow / Raise him a tombstone of snow." And then, chillingly, she writes in "Wife to Husband," "Pardon the faults in me, / For the love of years ago: / Good-bye. / I must drift across the sea, / I must sink into the snow, / I must die." She was never a wife: her one intended broke off their engagement, saying he wanted to become a priest. So I must imagine who this husband might be.

But perhaps I am misunderstanding her. Perhaps you are misunderstanding me. You may be thinking, all that snow is another word for obliteration, for the world wished away, for a kind of death. And perhaps you are right. It is I who misunderstands, and what I misunderstand is me.

But where I grew up, in north country, the first snow fell in mid-November and piled up, snow on snow (none of it melting, only clotting, becoming denser, withdrawing deeper to make room for more of itself) until March. And then the ticking would begin again, in droplets of meltwater, from eaves and tree branches, along gutters and downspouts, from the rust-gutted fenders and rocker panels of cars. Time tolls again, drip by drip, telling its beads. Hail Mary, Annunciated. Spring.

But her child will be born in the snow. And that, I think, is what I saw from my window: Him everywhere, snow on snow, snow on snow.

Robert Clark 37

I was cold and misunderstood and afraid to suffer, and as often as not that is how I seem to myself every December, sometimes every day.

Yet today is demonstrably cold, and somehow—for reasons I must misunderstand, on account of things I do not see—I am safe and warm. But for all that—just to be sure—I would like a bleak day, something to hope for, a promise to be fulfilled. So now from this other window, years and miles away, I am praying for snow.

JENNIFER DE LEON
Mapping Yolanda

One Friday night, the winter I was twelve, my mom's brother, Tío Erwin, showed up at my grandmother's apartment in Jamaica Plain with his new wife. She was fifteen. They'd met during his recent trip to Guatemala. She looked like any one of my cousins, only she didn't weigh as much. Her smile stretched, revealing teeth so white they looked like they'd glow in the dark. She was short like Tío, and had fluffy, frizzy hair, and her skin was the same color as the outside of a loaf of bread.

"This is Yolanda," Tío Erwin said. Underneath the buzzing fluorescent light in my grandmother's kitchen, he draped his arm over his bride's shoulder. They practically purred.

When I kissed Yolanda's cheek, I inhaled her scent—a combination of incense and floral perfume. She tickled my chubby middle and giggled when I stood back, startled. My mom tore the lid off a box of Dunkin' Donuts and set the box on the table where my aunts sat, their elbows resting on the green-and-white checkered tablecloth. "*Niños,*" she said. "*Váyanse para la sala!*" We were banned from the kitchen so the women could get to know Yolanda.

The living room was crowded with mustached uncles, including Tío Erwin, and my dad, who said, "*M'ija*" and pushed his lips toward the kitchen. *My daughter,* you should go play with your cousins.

Kids were forbidden from playing in the bedrooms too, so we were left with the linoleum strip of hallway. We cousins ranged in age from six-year-old David, a fan of Ninja Turtles, to sixteen-year-old Erika with her feathered bangs and Guns N' Roses T-shirts. Unlike most of my cousins, I adored Barbies and Pogo balls and puffy-painted tops. My sisters, parents, and I lived in a neighborhood where the only nighttime sound was a recycle bin rattling down a driveway.

My parents agreed that education was important. It was the reason they had left their homeland of Guatemala and, later, had abandoned Boston with its ethnic intimacy. They believed the suburbs meant security—good schools, organized sports, a library down the street. My mother pushed the idea of college on us before we could write in cursive. We took elective classes in French and read chapter books for fun. Many of my cousins, on the other hand, lived in Section 8 housing and changed schools often. But when we were all together, in the pocket of Friday night, we were the same. We played checkers and compared our favorite scenes in *The Goonies*. We played Go Fish with a sticky deck of cards. Eventually, we would teach Yolanda how to play too.

From where I sat that first night, cross-legged in the hallway next to the kitchen, I could see Yolanda's round face, mischievous grin, and nostrils wide as dimes. My grandmother sat closest to Yolanda, who was eating a Boston Kreme donut. Yolanda wore a long cotton skirt and a Celtics jacket. From my aunts' head nods and thick fingers raised in the air, it seemed someone was making a speech. I leaned closer and snatched what I could: *"uno nunca sabe...tiene que cuidarse."*

One never knows *what? You must take care of yourself.* They hadn't said be careful. That was something we constantly heard. Be careful riding the scooter, and don't go past the yellow house where the Chinese family lives. Be careful swimming or you might drown like Monica almost did one summer. *You must take care of yourself* implied a further concern. If you don't take care of yourself, then _____. Whatever filled that blank space, I wouldn't know for years.

That spring we celebrated my birthday with a barbecue at Larz Anderson Park. Surrounded by shades of green, my cousins and I were allowed to be as loud as we wanted without downstairs neighbors calling the cops to complain about *them spics*. I was thirteen, so I was too old to play tag. Instead I sat at the wooden picnic table and licked the salt off Cape Cod potato chips. I placed one on my tongue and let it dissolve like the wafer at Mass. Tío Erwin showed up again, this time without his teenage bride.

"Is Yolanda here?" he asked out of breath.

My mother ripped apart a head of iceberg lettuce and arranged the leaves onto a ceramic plate. "No."

Tío massaged his temples with his palms.

"She was gone when I woke up."

Later, we found out that Yolanda had been sleepwalking. I imagined her black jelly shoe sandals swishing past the triple-decker apartments, down the concrete hill, reaching Hyde Square, and headed to the supermarket or church. These were the only places she'd find someone to speak Spanish to, someone to tell about the baby kicking against her expanding belly. After that, Tío Erwin put newspapers on the rug next to her side of the bed so he'd hear if she got up in the middle of the night. Who knows where she would have wandered. My mother seemed especially concerned for Yolanda. Maybe it was because they had grown up in neighboring *colonias* in Guatemala. Or maybe she knew more than she would admit.

After the baby was born, Yolanda's mother, Doña Consuelos, arrived from Guatemala to help take care of her new grandson, Jonathan. Weeks and months stretched between family get-togethers— at least for me. Most weekends, I earned money babysitting, spending nights in wealthy people's living rooms. While their children slept, I tried to figure out the complicated remote controls to watch movies and eat endless snacks—Chipwiches in the freezer, Halloween candy in the cupboard all year round, pizza. I preferred these cushy tan couches where I could talk to friends on the phone to the crammed apartments in Boston where my parents and younger sister still spent weekend nights with family.

The minute I turned sixteen I started working at the Gap. I learned to fold jeans diagonally at the knee. I could explain the difference between classic and relaxed fit. The store manager called me Maria. Oh sorry, she'd say, looking over my head when I corrected her. With my employee discount I could finally afford the preppy styles displayed on the headless mannequins. I could fit in with the rich Jewish kids at my high school. My cousins started to call me *white girl*.

We branched out in different directions. Some of the guys took up weed and basketball or started having sex, and my girl cousins found love in the form of serious *novios*. Or they gained weight. My sister fulfilled my mother's lifelong dream and became the first in our extended family to go to college. I followed soon after, attending a small liberal arts school two hours away. College was like another country. They served food I'd never heard of (hummus), students wore clothes

I didn't have (Patagonia), and professors encouraged us to call them by their first names. At least I could speak the language, the middle-to-upper class, white, privileged vernacular—or at least I could fake it by throwing in the word *vicariously* now and then. A friend "couldn't believe" I'd never heard the song "Stairway to Heaven." I couldn't believe he had only two cousins. I had thirty-eight.

Once, in World Politics, a student in the front row with a blond ponytail and high-pitched voice declared that it was unjust for ATMs in America to offer Spanish as a language option. "Why don't people just learn to speak English?" The hardwood floors and ceiling-high windows closed in and I could feel eighty eyes on me. What did I have to say? Me, the Spanish-speaking representative in our classroom. I raised a shaking hand and said, "Sometimes it's easy to forget that the word *Florida* means 'flowered' in Spanish and that *Colorado* means 'red or colored'. These are words in Spanish because the Spanish were actually here before the English. I'm just saying."

When it became too much, when I simply grew tired of having to explain *where I'm from,* or when Mexican night in the college dining hall failed to soften my homesickness, I called my mother. Cell phones had not yet infiltrated campuses, but she had a special long-distance plan that allowed unlimited minutes on the weekend. Usually she spoke in Spanish and I used a mix of Spanish and English. When I didn't want my roommate to understand, I stuck to Spanish. My mother would ask about my classes and my friends and she would listen with enthusiasm. She'd catch me up on the family, almost always sharing news of a pregnancy, a separation, a scandal at church. One day, she called to tell me about Yolanda. I was sitting on my twin bed propped up by cinder blocks. My feet dangled off the edge, and through the window I could see that autumn had set the tops of trees ablaze in reds, oranges, and yellows.

"*Oye.* Yolanda called the cops on your Tío the other night. She was screaming, acting crazy. Tore at her own clothes, clawed her face with her nails. *Sí...*And she told the police that your Tío did it. They were going to arrest him but one of the police checked Yolanda's hands and found blood under her nails."

"Oh my God."

My roommate walked in wearing a bathrobe and holding a dorm shower caddy. "Who's pregnant now?"

"I'll call you back," I told my mom.

That winter, Tío Erwin, devastated, moved from Boston to Framingham with Jonathan, who was now in elementary school. No one saw Yolanda for a long time. If the adults still talked to her, I didn't know. Eventually, we lowered our heads at the mention of her name. She became hazy in my memory, nothing like the girl who tickled my middle in my grandmother's kitchen seven years before.

If I were to draw a timeline of my parents' lives, I could see that after they came to the United States in the seventies, their lives dramatically improved. They worked hard, saved money, and in the early eighties bought their first house. My mother learned to drive. We spent nearly every weekend visiting family in Boston, but we always returned to our house in Framingham on Sunday evenings in time for my sisters and me to finish our homework. But moving to the United States wasn't enough to guarantee a better life for Yolanda. It just wasn't that simple. She hadn't immigrated as we had. She had disappeared.

College came to an end. Classmates left for law school, medical school, fellowships, travel abroad, or jobs in New York City. I moved across the country to work as a teacher. I could have found a position in Framingham where my sixth-grade teacher still worked and still wore a beehive. Instead, I chose California. Deep down, I wanted to experience the feeling of being from somewhere else, of reaching for something more as my parents had done.

In San Jose, my third-grade students and their families came from Mexico or Vietnam. Names like *Nguyen, Tran, Le, Rodriguez,* and *Santiago* crammed the class roster. During a parent-teacher conference one afternoon, my student Andre, his father, mother, and three younger siblings, including an infant wrapped in a lavender blanket, shared the space opposite me at the kidney-bean-shaped table. Andre had the highest scores in the class. His mother wanted to know why he had misspelled *Halloween* on the last quiz. I wasn't sure if she was directing the question to Andre or to me.

"You know," his father said. "The price movie tickets in America too high." Andre's father was barely five feet tall. I wasn't much taller, but with heels I towered over him, so I was glad we were sitting down. "For me, my wife, and six, no, seven kids." He laughed. "We going to movies on weekend is spending over one hundred dollars."

I didn't know what to say. I tried to steer the conversation back to the Excel spreadsheet and Andre's test scores among national rankings.

"So I go Best Buy and purchase projector."

Andre's mother adjusted the sleeping infant in her arms. "What happens when a student misspells a word?"

"They must write the word ten times," I said. Who knew if it really worked?

"I go library and borrow DVDs. We play onto white wall of apartment," Andre's father said with a proud smile.

"Andre?" His mother called. He'd been playing with the other kids at the math station. "Come here and spell the word Halloween."

Andre stepped forward to display his mastery.

One week, a mother cried about her husband having been deported back to Mexico. The week after that, a mother fell asleep during our parent-teacher conference because she worked double shifts at night. The following month, another mother asked if I could help program her cell phone in Spanish. It was barely December of that first year of teaching and I'd already learned more about international relations than from any class in college. None of the readings on our syllabi described a situation like those of my students and their families. Or like those of lost Yolanda's. The women mentioned in our wordy textbooks were distant, statistical. Maybe that's why blond girls in ponytails so freely expressed their views on assimilation. But in those classrooms, we hadn't been discussing real people anyway, right?

I always knew that Yolanda, my parents, and other relatives hadn't moved from Guatemala to the United States for wanderlust, but it wasn't until I had moved away from Boston that I saw their stories in a different light. The flashbulbs of economics and politics had revealed realities, surely, but it was the stories of others—my students' families in particular—that started to unveil my own past, even my present.

To my surprise, during one of my trips home to Massachusetts, my mother suggested we visit Yolanda. She had turned up after all, had been in the vicinity all along, but lost to us. It had been years since I saw her. It was Christmas Day. We arrived at her run-down apartment building in Boston. What looked like urine and grease stained the sidewalk. Cars splashed through slush puddles along the one-way avenue. The air was cold and still. Graffiti marked up the bus stop signs. I breathed through my mouth to avoid the stench from the metal garbage can. The apartment buzzer didn't sound when I pushed it. All the other buttons were cracked or missing. My mom searched for pebbles on the ground and tossed a handful up to the second floor window, the sound of keys tapping on a typewriter.

"Yolanda! Open the door. It's Dora." She hesitated. "And Jennifer. She wants to say hi."

We were buzzed in. We stepped past the glass door and climbed the stairs. The muffled sound of a television filled the carpeted hall. We twisted our bodies so a man in a leather jacket coming down the staircase wouldn't knock us over. My mother tugged the sleeve of my black pea coat and said, "We're not going to stay long. I just want to see how she is."

We stood in front of her apartment door, wiping our boots on a welcome mat that was missing the *L* and *C*. WE OME. The door opened, and there was Yolanda, tucking her frizzy hair behind her ears. It was cut short, just above her shoulders. She'd gained weight. Maybe fifty pounds. Her red sweatshirt hugged tight around her hips and her stonewashed jeans belonged to another decade. My mother asked if she remembered me. She nodded.

"Come in," she said in a whisper. In the living room a wide-shouldered, dark-haired man was asleep on the couch. Yolanda made no introductions or explanations. Pieces of duct tape kept the blinds down along the windowsill. The space smelled of sleep. I stood close to my mother.

"Long time," Yolanda said squinting. "Let's go in the kitchen. Oh, yeah. *Feliz Navidad.*"

In the kitchen a little boy and girl sat on wooden chairs playing video games. The boy didn't look up, just clicked away at the neon screen. Chocolate milk splotches ran down the front of the little girl's pink sweatshirt. My mother baby-stepped her way over and slowly picked the girl up from under her arms, hugging her tight.

"My daughter," Yolanda said. "And that's my son." No one mentioned Jonathan.

Yolanda ordered them to share a seat and insisted we sit down, giving us each our own chair. Within seconds she was crying as if we'd just revealed terrible news.

"I know," my mother said. "It's OK."

I had no idea what they were talking about. Maybe I still believed I wasn't allowed to join the adults in the kitchen. Or maybe I didn't want to be part of this. It was easier, safer, to remain in the role of the child, my mother's daughter. Cowardly? Polite? I didn't know what to say to Yolanda anyway, so I stayed quiet, looked around the room. The kids wore mismatched socks. Dishes cluttered the counters. A Mass Health magnet secured a child's drawing of a butterfly to the refrigerator. I felt far away—not only from all this, but strangely, far away from myself.

We didn't stay long. On our way out, my mother slipped Yolanda a twenty-dollar bill, not because she asked, but because that was and still is the kind of thing my mother does. In the car, my mother said that even with sun and rain, some fruit still falls, still spoils.

Some days after our visit with Yolanda in her cavelike apartment, I heard that she had attacked her mother who was still living with her, helping with the two new children as she had with Jonathan. Yolanda tried to stab her with a pair of scissors. The state took away Yolanda's kids and she was admitted to a mental health institution. I never saw her again.

Two years later I came home to Boston for good. Once home, I felt the absence of my cousins who had moved away. Some followed work—Texas, California, Indiana. Others followed war—Iraq, Afghanistan, North Carolina in between. One was serving time. Most of the girls had had babies. We were all spread out, moving farther away from that linoleum strip of hallway in our grandmother's walk-up. Even as adults, we cousins remained the children of parents who wanted more from life and who believed that moving to America would achieve it. Moving was upward—at least in our minds. Our stories might begin and end in a different place, but we inherited the belief that leaving was part of the formula for economic progress. But now I sense that the reason for departure is as important as the destination. Yolanda wasn't purely seeking more opportunities in the United States; she was trying to escape the past.

Years later at my parents' house, I finally asked my mother to fill in the gaps of Yolanda's story, a narrative that began long before the day she had arrived in Boston. My mother was sitting at the dining room table sewing the hem on a pair of my jeans. "She was so young," she said.

I stared at the impressionist painting on the opposite wall. A café in Paris. A framed print my mother had picked up at a yard sale.

"Yolanda was only fourteen, not fifteen, when she came."

What other details, I wondered, had my mother smudged from the past.

"As a girl," she explained, "Yolanda helped her mother clean the rooms at a brothel. She'd been raped."

I was thankful for the sudden noise of the needle, stitching at a high speed.

My mother used her teeth to cut a loose piece of thread. "She was still a girl when she left for the United States with your Tío. Imagine."

"How did they meet?"

"On the street."

I cleared my throat.

"Not like that. Everyone hangs out on the street there. It's not like here. Your Tío was in Guatemala and Doña Consuelos saw that he was a good man."

"So, that's it? A good man is hanging out on the street and you send your teenage daughter to live with him in another country?"

"Things are different there."

My uncle was a prince on a white horse—or a prince with a blue passport. Maybe Yolanda's mother hoped that sending her daughter to the United States would give her a new beginning, the kind that could even delete the past. But it hadn't. When Doña Consuelos moved to Boston to help with Jonathan, she seemed only to make things worse. Her presence probably ignited painful memories for Yolanda.

"We didn't know how to help her."

I welcomed the hypnotic hum of the sewing machine. We have no control over the circumstances into which we are born. The ropes we reach for in trying to soar somewhere new, somewhere better, often carry us to unpredictable places. How would Yolanda's life have played out had she never left Guatemala, how would my mother's have turned out if she hadn't either? In all the stories she told about the small Central American country that would be the source of comparison for everything my sisters and I ate, wore, and read, she was teaching us about the world and to appreciate what we had.

"Here." She handed me the jeans and placed her elbows on the table the way my aunts had done that first night Yolanda had arrived at my grandmother's apartment in Boston.

"Thanks," I said.

As I folded them at the knee, I could just see Yolanda with her frizzy hair, seated at another table somewhere, playing cards in a pale-painted room, and with her mischievous smile, saying, Go fish, go fish.

PATRICIA FOSTER
Inside

I'm staring at a rush of players on the screen—fragments of knees and shoulders, a collision of helmets—when the two aides in front of me leap from their seats and yell, "Go go go," as if they're rallying with fans under a blue dome of sky rather than with patients in pajamas and robes in the dayroom, a dank smell of sweat and antiseptic thickening the air. It's a late Saturday afternoon. To my right, Floyd leans forward, slack-jawed, nodding at the TV. He's a middle-aged man with Down Syndrome and depression, and though I don't want to, I can't seem to avoid seeing his butt crack and the way his ball cap presses tight against his dark, greasy hair. Beside him Susie lies quietly in her lounger, frantically knitting and separating her hands as if she's learning how to clap. "Help me help me help me," she mutters in a low, rhythmic chant, barely audible.

While the nurses and aides seem mesmerized by the game, I sit on a wobbly plastic chair at the back of the room beside my husband. I glance at him. Without taking his eyes from the screen, he reaches over and puts his hand in mine. How much longer? I wonder. How much longer will we be inside?

It had seemed so simple: in and then out, a voluntary admission. And yet, when Jay decided to admit himself, I was surprised. Then again, depression can become unbearable, even unmanageable, a thick, bewildering fog, heavy with defeat. "Two or three days at the most," Dr. L, the psychiatric resident at the university hospital said yesterday over the phone about Jay's possible hospitalization, a course of action he strongly recommended. When Jay agreed, I was hopeful. For the past two months, I'd felt the weight of his depression, heavy enough to make our household sag. His moods had become a cloudy mixture of fretful anxiety and blurred desire, and because he was mired in sadness and uncertainty, he turned to me at every obstacle: *Should he change his diet, perhaps eat less meat or give up dairy or take more Omega 3 or stop worrying about the whole damn thing? Should he turn off the cable and thus save us money or keep it on with the hope of occasional entertainment? Would I please stop asking him if he was OK?* I was tired, full of anxieties myself. I wanted him to right what was wrong.

That afternoon as we packed Jay's bag, I emptied one of his pockets of wadded up paper, straightening it out in my hand, and thought idly that this was the conceit for what the hospital would do: take a crumpled piece of paper and carefully smooth it out. Looking back, the metaphor now seems ludicrous. But I thought then that the progression from lingering depression to "ordinary unhappiness," as Freud termed normalcy, would be a quick fix.

But on that chilly, gray afternoon in November when the spidery limbs of trees were not yet coated with snow, I was still naïve. Jay and I took the elevator to the second floor of the university hospital, walked down a long beige hall, turned right into another beige hall and there it was: the locked ward.

Waiting for the nurse to buzz us in, it seemed like a cliché, a scene played out in hundreds of movies and books I'd read. I felt ridiculous thinking of Jack Nicholson strung out on his bed, helpless and weak after ECT treatments in *One Flew Over the Cuckoo's Nest* or the pale, flabby Esther Greenwood, lying lethargic and fat after insulin treatments in Sylvia Plath's *The Bell Jar*. I waved these images aside. Jay was going in for two days, maybe three, to have his medication adjusted, to engage in what the intern had called "aggressive therapy," seeing a psychiatrist daily. It sounded benign.

Then the nurse opened the door and all I heard was a loud insistent moaning, *anngh, anngh, anngh, anngh,* a syllabic monotone, constant and greedy, that tightened the stomach and grated on the nerves, followed by a high-pitched "help me help me help me" floating in the overcooled air. I wanted to laugh. *My god, the loony bin!* And yet no one else seemed to pay the least bit of attention to these sounds or to the woman creeping, with her walker, down the hall, a blue plastic bag full of clothes looped over one arm, her face hidden by strands of long, gray hair. I pretended not to look.

At the nurses' station, I had no choice: three elderly people lay before me on loungers, their faces slack in medicated sleep, tangled hair flat on their heads, gowns and robes askew. Another man, in a dark blue ball cap, sat at a computer table, grinning at nothing. When he flashed that empty grin at me, I smiled back, but he shifted his gaze just above my head. I glanced away, only to be arrested by a man's emaciated legs—pale and hairless, fish-belly white under the fluorescent lights—draped over the armrest of a lounger. I realized that Jay had been placed in the geriatric unit, a fact I noted casually. After all, he'd be seeing Dr. L and his regular therapist, both of whom he'd seen at this hospital just the day before. This would all be sorted out.

"Well now," the nurse said to Jay. "We'll need for you to undress. We have to search your clothes"—she smiled—"and then we'll give them back to you."

Standing alone in the hall while my husband undressed in front of a male nurse in another room, I felt as conspicuous, as baffled and terrified as the new kid at school. What in hell were we doing here?

But I knew. At least, I knew the facts. More than a year ago Jay had been diagnosed with Bipolar II, a subtype of manic depression, a condition defined by mildly elevated moods and episodic depressions. His diagnosis had been like a bright light, a flash of recognition at his revved-up energy, his bursts of talk, his impulsive, compelling actions followed by flashes of irritability—don't *bother* me, he'd snap if I interrupted him while he was writing an e-mail—and then the sudden slouch into exhaustion and days of watching TV. His study often seemed a microcosm of his mood swings: in the middle of a project, his room resembled a disaster zone with papers and magazines in piles all over the floor mingling with dirty clothes, Coke cans, half-filled coffee cups, plates with paper napkins stuck to sticky forks or spoons. I'd pick one up. Could that have been almond butter? Raspberry jam? I wasn't sure. Once liberated from his project, he'd go to Office Depot, buy six big plastic crates with snap-on tops and in a flurry of tidiness, separate the trash from the claimed, sweep the floor and finally take out two yard bags full of garbage to be picked up on Wednesday.

For a year he'd been on high doses of an antidepressant and had spent hours with a wonderful therapist who helped him see his own desires more clearly, a process that made him more hopeful but also more vulnerable, all his nerve endings exposed. "I'm fine and then, well, suddenly I'm capsizing," he told me one night as we sat together on the couch in the dark, our knees touching, our heads resting on separate pillows. Until two years ago, he'd had no debilitating depressions, had so rarely seemed "down" that I thought of myself as the more anxious partner, the one on the verge of disintegration. After all, for twenty years, he'd gone to work every day, caffeinated and curious (if no longer impassioned by his job), taken Friday nights off to cook dinner and watch movies with me, planted tulips in early November and shoveled the sidewalks in winter, even though he hated doing it. Then, in late 2008, as if we'd been living in a dual-career fantasy world, the economy crashed and Jay's company laid him off. In the snap of someone's fingers, he was a man over fifty without work.

Within months, he slipped hard and fast into a depression.

"You need anything?" one of the nurses asked after Jay redressed and we "moved" into his sunless room, a space so spare, so empty of hope I wanted only to close the door and walk away.

"Oh, I'd like to have my cookies," Jay said. To my surprise, he'd brought chocolate chip cookies from home. "And some coffee would be terrific," he joked, pretending he was ordering room service.

"Sure," the nurse said. "I'll just cruise down to Starbucks in the lobby and get you a double espresso."

I thought she was kidding, but to my surprise, she did just that. Jay and I looked at each other. *Service!* Another nurse stopped in to show Jay the menu choices for the next day and to make sure he was comfortable. "Don't get the pizza," she said drolly, "unless you like, well, flavored cardboard." She seemed funny, sardonic, a gift of the hospital, one of those women who makes you feel normally weird instead of just weird. Maybe being *inside* wasn't going to be so bad: friendly nurses, magazines, Starbucks coffee. Most important, he could call me anytime during the day.

"And you can stay *all day* if you want," the nurse said, turning to me. "*What?*"

She pointed to the visiting hours: 10:00 a.m.–10:00 p.m.

Another surprise. I was inside too. Inside included me too.

*

That evening, I walked into the quiet of our house, expecting to spend the next few days catching up on work and sleep. I'd just finished an exhausting literary conference, had been so busy that I'd forgotten to call my sister on her birthday, a lapse that would demand sack cloth and flagellation. Now, more than anything, I wanted to be alone and undisturbed. Yet, sitting at my kitchen table, what I felt wasn't relief at all but a nagging guilt that some part of me had applauded this act, had longed to be released from worrying about Jay and the intractable mysteries of depression. I'd imagined squandering languorous hours on myself, wandering idly around the house as my tea steeped, letting my mind roam to a little Czech town in Alabama where I was thinking about setting a novel. I'd assumed that I'd see Jay for an hour in the late afternoon. I'd thought that the psychiatric ward would be hermetic, sealed, his little kingdom of necessary retreat. And that's what I'd have too: a retreat.

But I found myself brooding about Jay at that small, bare hospital table, everything made safe and functional and bland. At least dirt and mess suggested action, a personality at work. I imagined Jay turning on his iPod or opening up *The New Yorker* or *Rolling Stone* as he tried to suppress the instinct to flee. *I* had wanted to flee that same creepy room.

It was more than the aesthetics of the place. I sensed, but couldn't yet articulate, a diagnostic difference that might put me in opposition to Jay's keepers. Jay was on suicide watch—we'd both spied (how could we not?) the little security camera aimed coyly at his bed—because Dr. L, the admitting physician, had thought Jay depressed enough to be suicidal. Jay insisted that he wasn't, and I believed him.

"I haven't gone to that place," he'd told me the night before as we sat together on the couch. He tightened his hand in mine. "I'll tell you if I do." His voice was quiet, almost a whisper. "I promise that."

Now as I sat at the kitchen table eating a slice of buttered toast, I remembered something else he'd said. "I know that somewhere inside me is the self I recognize. I…I just can't get to him right now." *Jay*. What I saw in my husband was a man whose faith in himself—

his identity, his goodness—had succumbed to self-doubt. What the doctors saw, I feared, was a diagnostic category, a gloss of symptoms, a mood disorder that could be corrected by medication.

Surely we'd hash out these ideas tomorrow when Dr. L met with Jay.

The next morning Dr. K, a large, matronly woman, marched into Jay's room with another woman, an intern, in tow. She introduced herself as the psychiatrist who would be assessing and treating Jay, and then introduced her intern. "I'm her boss," she said peremptorily, as if hierarchy *was* Dr. K's identity.

I'd been sitting in one of the two available chairs in the room, talking to Jay about a graduate class I was teaching. Oh, wait a minute, I thought. *Wait.* Where is Dr. L? But as Dr. K spoke, I realized I knew her, had served with her on a dissertation committee years before, where she'd been an outside committee member, and for a fleeting instant, I felt relief. I remembered her as a benign presence, a bit awkward in our discussion of narrative craft, but someone who seemed smart and observant, chiming in when a chapter involved geriatric medicine.

"I think we know each other," she said, as if reading my thoughts. "It was…oh, that *ridiculous* thesis…a dreadful piece of work." She frowned, her mouth tightening, then reminded me that she'd spent time on "that side of the river (the humanities; she also had a PhD), but it's impossible to live on the pay."

Hardly a fact that I, low on the ladder of humanities salaries in English, was in a position to argue. But I was most conscious of her attention to me—chatting about a mutual colleague—while Jay, her patient, sat on the bed in hospital robe and slippers, ignored and waiting. She gazed so intently at me that I straightened as if I, too, were under examination, as if my sanity and instincts were also being judged. I stared at her narrowed eyes—was that a predatory gaze?—at her stiff, white coat and sensed a controlling nature disguising, perhaps, an ingrown inferiority. Didn't I know something of those dark streets of academia? The frayed psychological temperament of the better-paid sciences was looking a lot like the sad humanities as I gazed back at her.

When Dr. K finally turned to Jay, she peered impatiently at him in his frumpy hospital garb, the robe uneven, his hair still uncombed, flat on one side, and stated, bluntly, that his file noted he was suicidal. "And I noticed that you haven't been participating in the normal activities of the hospital." He started to speak, but she raised her hand. "You didn't have breakfast with the other patients this morning, and you haven't dressed, haven't interacted with anyone in the dayroom."

Instinctively, I edged forward in my seat, gazing out at the men and women lying on the loungers in the dayroom: here were bodies worn down, made smaller perhaps by the low pulse of despair and old age. I'd been here for over an hour and I had yet to hear a patient say anything other than the constant refrain of "help me help me help me."

"I had blood drawn this morning," Jay said. He sounded, I couldn't help but notice, defensive. I wanted suddenly to smooth his hair, to tidy his robe. "My breakfast tray didn't come until at least an hour after everyone else's."

She nodded.

"And quite frankly, I didn't know I was *supposed* to dress. I've been sitting here reading." He held up the latest issue of *The New Yorker*.

After acknowledging that such reading might be of interest to him personally, Dr. K insisted that because depression could make one isolate oneself, getting well meant participating socially and emotionally with others.

I wanted to laugh, to say, "Oh, come on. Let's not *play* this game." But her voice was so gravely serious, her tone so quietly disapproving that I saw she believed that sitting on the couch and watching TV with elderly, medicated patients would be therapeutic.

"I don't feel suicidal," Jay said. "I feel depressed, but not suicidal."

Dr. K looked at her notes. "The referring physician thought you were. And the nurse last night said you talked of suicide."

Jay glanced sheepishly at me. "I was talking to her about the way I felt over a year ago. It's true, I did feel suicidal then. I thought I made that clear. She was talking about a time when *she* felt suicidal."

My stomach tightened. Already I could see how Jay's natural tendency toward honesty, his need to talk, to empathize, to create a story with transitions and layered meanings might entrap him here.

"Well, my gut feeling is that you're still at risk. The highest rates of suicide are in older white males. That's not my opinion. That's a fact. I think you will need to stay in this unit anywhere from one week to one month." She glanced at me as if she were finished with Jay. "I don't think he will be getting any night passes for a while. I will recommend day passes rather soon so that he can go to other parts of the hospital and have more freedom, but no night passes for at least a week."

"But," he protested, "this was a *voluntary* admission."

She turned her attention back to him. "Yes, it was, but you need to trust me on this." She smiled a tight, detached smile. She seemed to loom above us even as she sat in the chair by the desk. "If you had a manuscript to be read and you wanted an expert opinion, you'd ask your wife to do that rather than ask me, wouldn't you?"

My husband nodded, uncertain where this was going. "The same can be said for your treatment. I'm very well trained."

An icy chill spread through my body. How often has "well-trained" been used as an authoritarian nod to credentials as control? This woman clearly wanted my husband—and me—to surrender to her authority, but did she also want me to witness my husband's humiliation? To be complicit with it?

"They told us it would only be a two- or three-day stay," I said, my voice rising despite my attempt to be calm. "Jay *agreed* with that stipulation…I don't understand."

"Well, I think it will be longer." Now she turned to Jay.

For a moment he looked defiant—his jaw clenched, his arms crossed—ready to protest her perceptions, but then as suddenly, his face slackened, his arms loosened, and to my surprise, he nodded.

What, I wanted to ask, is going on here? But now I, too, felt confused, addled by what had just happened. Did Jay want to stay? Had he changed his mind, perceived some tenuous thread of hope I'd missed? Was there something I'd misunderstood?

After ten minutes, I left so that Dr. K could talk privately with him.

Although a longer stay inside might be part of Dr. K's professional opinion, it seemed off-kilter. Her insistence on Jay's psychological condition was based on notes from Dr. L, an intern who had seen him once for less than forty minutes, and the tattling of a night nurse.

Dr. K's treatment strategy of enforced participation with patients unable to carry on the most elemental of conversations was clearly absurd. But more than that, I sensed in her a difficult, withholding temperament, a woman who would not like Jay's associative, ironic point of view. Although I'd been raised to trust a doctor's skills, I didn't trust hers. I kept remembering the way she looked at Jay with her steady gaze, her eyes slightly magnified by rimless glasses, eyes that showed no warmth, no deep interest, and I wondered if she preferred geriatric medicine because so many of the patients, at least in this ward, seemed inarticulate and helpless.

I walked into the kitchen, filled the kettle with water, and stood by the stove, thinking. The doctor. What did I really know of her? Nothing. Or nothing much. All I had were flashes of perception and an urgent grip of fear at the power she possessed to keep Jay inside. And yet somewhere beneath my apprehension lurked a buried memory, a shadowy scratching. *What?* I sat with my cup of tea, waiting. Outside, the sky was clearing, the grayness dissolving. The trees, though bare, looked less forlorn, the branches almost touching the windows. And in this idle moment, it came to me.

A few years ago, a colleague and I had been walking her dog along the side streets of our town, talking about our students and our writing. My colleague had been telling me about a young, brilliant student who had written an essay about her father's suicide. Startled now by the suddenness of this memory, I felt another shiver of fear. The student was Dr. K's daughter. Was I remembering it right? Did Dr. K's husband commit suicide? If it was true, then it made more sense that after such an experience Dr. K would see my husband—maybe even most people— as "at risk." It made sense that she'd want to protect him, to ensure his safety. Then again, I thought unkindly, maybe she drove her husband to it. Or maybe he'd made her life miserable, had been the sort of bullying husband who left scars and irreconcilable pain. I had no clue.

I knew only that my husband was not her husband.

Immediately I called both Dr. L and Jay's therapist, but it was a late Friday afternoon and I got their answering machines. Then I called my colleague to confirm what I'd remembered about our conversation from years before.

*

"There's something wrong here," Jay said when he called from the hospital. Now he sounded angry and offended, anything but compliant. "It doesn't matter what I say about my state of mind. It's more or less assumed that patients' views aren't to be trusted, so there's no reason for me to discuss what I consider the nuances of my feelings and behavior. It's as if I'm here to be watched and directed and medicated. *That's all.*"

"We need to get you out of there," I said. "There's something spooky going on, something that I don't think has anything to do with you. Or not enough anyway."

"Can she keep me here?" For the first time I heard panic in his voice.

"I don't think so." It had never occurred to me to ask such a pointed question on that whirlwind day when Jay decided to commit himself.

Although I couldn't get in touch with Jay's doctors, I planned to check Jay out tomorrow, the third day. At least this was my opinion until I talked to my sister, an internist in practice for over thirty years. "You can leave," she told me, "but if you do so without the doctor's approval, you'll be labeled AMA (Against Medical Advice) and your insurance won't pay."

As I listened, the weight of my fear shifted. I couldn't speak.

"What you need to do is convince the doctor that Jay is using the insights about medication and sleep he's gained while in the hospital to structure the next three or four weeks of his time. He'll also need confirmed visits with a shrink, so you've got to request a meeting with the attending psychiatrist."

You must convince *her.*

You must convince her.

Now I was really frightened. To calm myself, I ran a bath full of hot water, letting the warmth and moisture relax my thighs and hips and chest. I closed my eyes, imagining my dread dissolving in the humid air.

I lay in bed that night, listening to the clatter of wooden blinds against the windowsill in a rush of wind. Perhaps it was the rhythmic knocking of the blinds or the charged repetition of my thoughts that made me sit up in the empty dark, my toes stiffening, my knees locked. *We can't do this alone.* I yanked off the sheet and tried to soften my heels, flex my instep, but my body refused to relax. Who would help us?

In the morning, I went over my options. The Patient Advocacy Office at the hospital was closed over the weekend. Likewise, the hospital insurance office. My own insurance carrier would not be available until Monday. This meant I couldn't resolve my concerns about insurance should we leave the hospital AMA today. I wanted to call Dr. K and request a meeting, but there was no direct way to approach her except by calling the ward and leaving a message. *You must convince her.* I let the steam from my tea warm my face, the cup held close to my cheek. And then I picked up the phone and called the hospital administrator on duty, the highest ranking doctor I could think of, to request a meeting with Dr. K. More than anything I wanted for us to talk directly to her, but without external intervention I feared such a meeting would be fruitless, a repetition of yesterday. After talking to several layers of bureaucracy, I was finally connected with a social worker who assured me my request for a meeting would be honored.

Two hours later Jay and I were sitting in the day room beside the other patients. Shaved and dressed in day clothes, Jay talked quietly to the man with Down Syndrome. Jay seemed oddly calm. When Dr. K came into the ward, she glanced at us and then disappeared into a patient's room. Just seeing her, I knew what really frightened me: if I couldn't persuade her to release Jay, then I'd have failed my husband. I imagined the worst: her refusal to let Jay leave; Jay's sudden snap of anger; her order for drugs to calm him, tranquilizing drugs that would put him in a stupor on the dayroom couch, nodding off with the rest of the patients while his normal life swam out of sight. I knew that Jay had both more maturity and more insight than to be overcome by fear, but still I worried.

But this wasn't only about Jay. Was it possible I wanted to be, if not Dr. K, at least a woman with her command? I stared out the window at the gray November sky, at the cars lined up at the stoplight, their windows rolled up, the radio probably on. I envied them.

An ordinary day. Going to the grocery store. Taking a child to violin lessons. Arguing with a spouse about the phone bill. There, mingled with my anxiety, was my old friend, self-pity. Poor me! I watched a branch tap against the window. Tap, tap, tap. A small breath of hope.

An hour passed. "I'll see you right after my next patient," Dr. K said.

Once in Jay's room, the three of us were watchful, knowing that something would be decided. Jay sat on the bed, I on a chair, Dr. K on the chair by the desk. She looked imperious, graceless, alone. Alone in her own skin, alone on the ward except for these sad, elderly patients. None of the nurses or aides talked easily or laughed with her as I'd seen them do with other doctors coming and going more often; they turned away, got very busy with paperwork or a patient when she strode into the ward so that she was always set apart, her authority intact. That's what would be important: her authority must not seem to slip into shadow. Our appeal would require finesse. I looked quickly at Jay, thinking about the plan we'd discussed.

"I want to leave today," Jay began, calm and focused. His white shirt was tucked in, his khaki pants barely wrinkled. "I've had no reaction to the medication for three days, and I've talked with my therapist, the one I've been working with for over a year. He's assured me that he'll have an appointment available for me on Monday."

Dr. K nodded as if she understood, then she smiled a small, superior smile and placed both hands flat on his chart. "But your therapist is not a psychiatrist, Jay. He's a psychologist and that's a person with a PhD but not a medical degree. To assure your continued treatment, you still need to be seen by a psychiatrist."

We understood the definitions, but I could see how smugly she'd stated her point.

"What about Dr. L?" Jay asked.

"I'm not sure Dr. L will be available," she said.

"We would like for you to check on that," I added. "We know you're terribly busy but this is important to us. We'd like for Jay to have an appointment next week."

When she looked at me, her gaze was no longer friendly, but for the first time I didn't feel afraid.

Then Jay spoke. "I feel like I've achieved what I intended to achieve by coming here," he said, his words so scripted, so unlike his own ironic voice that I wanted to laugh. "I've adjusted well to the new medication, and I'm to increase it incrementally over the next two weeks. I'm aware that I must pay attention to sleep, and I have the sleep medication you ordered if I need it. I'm to check in with Dr. L..." he continued in his new patient voice, the one that said "the rules, the rules, good Lord, see how I'm obeying the rules." And now if you'll be so very kind as to withdraw your tentacles.

She looked at Jay, at me. "I don't advise this," she said brusquely. She started to stand but then she didn't. I saw a slight flicker of uncertainty as she glanced down at Jay's chart. "I see you went to the Self-Esteem group today." She looked up.

"Yes," he said, meeting her gaze with a pleasant nod. "I did."

"Good," she said. "I'll have to think about this. As I said, it isn't what I prefer, but I'll see what I can do."

And then she left us there. Could we possibly have won?

Late afternoon. Jay and I stare at the football players huddled together on TV. An hour earlier, Dr. K provisionally agreed to discharge Jay "with reservations" at the end of the day. Now we wait. She has not yet signed the papers. The door is still locked. We watch the players move back and forth across the field as if any of it matters. During a lull in the game, I hear again the scraping sound of the rubber-tipped walker as the woman with the blue bag approaches the doorway. Jay must hear it too. His head turns. Discreetly, I shift my posture so that I can glance in that direction. To my surprise the woman is looking directly at Jay, her gaze steady. He nods, acknowledging something between them, affirming some small but inevitable link they share, an unspoken allegiance that being here is part of being human. As if steadied by his look, her gaze becomes so naked, so private, so full of an unfathomable grief that I feel like a trespasser on the ground they share. Grateful for the roar from the TV, I turn to watch a player lift his hands into the air and catch a beautiful, spiraling pass. When I glance back to the door, the hallway is empty. The scrape-scrape-scrape of the walker can still be heard, but the woman has moved on.

Patricia Foster

LYNN FREED
Gloria Mundi

Sometimes, after my daily dose of radiation, I would stop at a small bath store near the hospital to buy a bar of soap, perhaps, or a bottle of bath gel. I liked the little shop; it was holding its own among the retro hippie emporia of the neighborhood, no hint yet of tea tree or patchouli or tie-dye.

Looking back on that time now, I wonder whether I was drawn to soaps and gels because, unlike, say, a belt or a pair of shoes, they could be counted upon not to outlast me. I don't know; I didn't go in search of a belt or shoes, and was in no mood for metaphors of mortality.

Down in the radiation suite, beyond natural light, it was as if a scrim had been lifted, revealing a just perspective on everything. I would look with keen interest at the other victims, wondering whether, like me, they had come to a new understanding, an acceptance—at times, even a celebration—of the temporal nature of all things.

Which was not to say I had not always known that nothing lasts. My twelve years in an Anglican school in South Africa had built in daily reminders of the impermanence of the things of this earth. So, too, did the poetry we read, the histories, the Bible itself. I would listen, I would read, I would understand. And then, when school was over, I would go back into my life, feeling immortal.

Still, as a Jew, I rather envied Christians their faith in an afterlife. Every morning, in prayers, we sang hymns, glorious hymns, Heaven all around us. "Everything shall perish away," sang our Zulu maid, daughter of a Methodist minister, with a lusty cheerfulness that made perishing away seem like joyful anticipation.

But for me, peddling off to Hebrew School three afternoons a week, there was no such assurance. Jews, as I came to understand it, didn't pay much attention to Heaven; when we died, it seemed, we disappeared. What did matter was to remember our earthly history, to observe our laws, and, never mind what the Almighty allowed to happen to us, to praise, glorify, exalt, and extol Him regardless—He-whose-name-was-so-terrible-it-was-never-to-be-uttered.

Meanwhile, my mind would wander away into the future, that time that seemed so slow in coming, when all this would be over, school and Hebrew school both, and I'd be free. But to be what, I would wonder? And where? And how? And even though I knew that the Almighty tended to smite those who disobeyed His laws, being smitten didn't worry me too much, sitting there on that hard bench with other fractious and smelly children, all of us worn out after a long day of it.

So, I would stare out the window in what I took to be His direction and implore Him to get me through this and out into the real world as quickly as possible. If He did, I promised, I would praise, glorify, exalt, and extol Him every day of my life. *Sh'ma Yis'ra'eil Adonai Eloheinu Adonai echad.*

But then, out of nowhere, could come a thought to make my heart jump in terror: at any moment, death itself might snatch away my mother or my father. It had happened to others, it could happen to me. And for this even the thought of Heaven would provide no comfort. I wanted both of them here, on earth, alive, and if someone had to die first, I wanted it to be me. Then, at least, there would be no question of being left behind.

And so I kept a firm eye on them, taking comfort from their insouciance in the face of life's terrors as I saw them—doors left wide open to the night, windows too—and even from the way my father drove, like a madman, cornering on two wheels, pushing the old DeSoto to 108 mph on the open road.

When, finally, he did die, not in a car crash but, at the age of eighty-five, from lung cancer, still I was left—quite adult now, quite mindful of mortality—more shocked, more desolate and bowed down than I might have been as a child. It was as if childhood itself had died with him, home as well—a childhood and a home that, without thinking, I had counted on to carry me through to the end.

Then, a year after his death, anomalies showed up on a routine mammogram. Biopsies followed, blood tests, MRIs, CT scans, X-rays, a lumpectomy, and six weeks of radiation. People who claim to know how one thing leads to another had no doubt of cause and effect: some were for the death of my father, others for a divorce I'd battled through some years before. Stress, grief, loss—these were the words invoked when laying blame for an illness whose cause was (and remains) unknown.

But grief is not a cigarette, and neither is stress. And none of the remedies offered by the grief-and-stress brigade—meditation, yoga, exercise, "mindfulness," supplements, diets of every description—none of these seemed able to turn me from a person who worried things through to someone who could take things as they came.

Nor, I found, my brush with mortality notwithstanding, was I to be transformed from someone who could take pleasure in a bar of triple-milled French soap and, over time, in more enduring purchases—a pair of sandals, perhaps, linen sheets, an Indian miniature painted on ivory, an antique ivory doctor's doll—into an ascetic, or at least someone who would consider shopping trivial in light of the greater scheme of things.

And if, once the radiation was over, the purchases I began to make again were to outlive me, I could take pleasure even in this. In fact, the whole idea of transience took hold of me like a sort of rapture. *Sic transit gloria mundi,* we had learned in school. *Memento mori.* "Look on my works, ye Mighty, and despair!" we'd recited. "Ah! Vanitas Vanitatum!" we'd read, "Which of us is happy in this world? Which of us has his desire? Or, having it, is satisfied?"

And though, at the age of fifteen or sixteen, I understood quite well the truth and scope of Thackeray's words, ambitious as I was and wild for life, I enjoyed an unquestioning faith that the things I desired, both material and immaterial, would deliver a measure of satisfaction. Satisfaction, delight, hope—even the choosing of a new pencil box at the start of a school year could bring fresh immediacy to life.

It was with just such hope that, more than forty years later, the radiation treatments behind me, I went in search of something new to wear for an upcoming book tour. What I wanted was a change of look, something in keeping with the wisdom I thought I'd acquired during the soap-buying times. The writing of the book itself had straddled the long vigil over my father's dying, and I had finished it just before the offending mammogram. So now, a year later, there I was again, with what felt like familiar purpose, back at the racks, the shelves, the dressing rooms of desire.

My mother had practiced just such purposefulness when she was out on a hunt, clipping along in her stockings and heels, mouth set, watch consulted, as if the whole business of shopping were to be put behind her with dispatch so that the real work of the day—a play to stage, a cast to assemble—could begin.

But she didn't fool me. I knew perfectly well that shopping was work too, joyful work. To search among the limited offerings available in a far-flung country—to go in search of, say, an evening dress in which to take a bow, something classic that would endure when the fashions changed, or a good pair of Italian shoes, ditto, Sanderson linen for the lounge curtains that had perished in the sun, and, if there was time, to hurry down the lane to the little antique shop where Mr. Potts, who lent her props for her stage productions in return for an ad in the program, might be persuaded to lower the price on a lovely Georgian cigarette box, because how many years had they known each other? she would ask him, and then turn away to examine a pair of silver grape scissors so that he had time to consider—to spend a morning like this and then come away in triumph was to breathe the very oxygen of life.

The fact is objects of desire have always seemed to bring with them what I can only think of as promise for the future—not only in the having but also in the seeking of them. And if the search produces nothing, or if, once something is found, the promise turns to dust after a day or so, well, still there has been the sport of it, the anticipation, the pounce, the triumph over the deadening brake of common sense.

And yet, having made it back onto a real shopping street after all those months of abstinence, I felt as if unmoored. There I stood in front of a three-way mirror, trying too hard to love the look of myself in a breathtakingly expensive designer suit. I had chosen it over all natural inclination, but, somehow, the new way of seeing life had left me unable to see myself in any familiar way. Or even to dismiss the sales lady's loud approval, which would once have left me untouched. "Understated," she said, circling, "Timeless." And, staring at myself in the three-way mirror, pale and rather thin, I wished, oh, I wished that my mother were not old and demented or, even if she were, that her astral spirit were there to say to me, "Darling, take it off, it makes you look like an undertaker."

But she was not there, and, forgetting completely that I had never warmed much to understatement, and certainly not to the timelessness of mud green, I bought the suit, and wore it a few times during the book tour in the spirit of a cross-dressing undertaker. And then, when the tour was over, I retired it to the back of my wardrobe, where, happily, moths found it, making it easier to throw out when the time came.

And although the times for throwing out began to bank up more regularly—to take hold, in fact, as a sort of ideal—on the shopping streets themselves I was returning to myself. Strolling in and out of the shops, it was as if I'd never suffered any sobering reminders of perishing away for all the rapidity with which hope could return at the sight, say, of a cheerfully lined basket, marked down now because the overpriced little French boutique was going out of business.

I stared at it. Another basket? Was I not already rich in baskets? But if I was, so what? Almost every night now I woke in panic, 2 a.m., 3 a.m., alone in the darkness. *Timor mortis conturbat me,* I would tell myself, *Our pleasance here is all vain glory.*

What, then, in the greater scheme of things, could a French basket matter? This small pleasure? This brief dart of hope?

Nothing, that I knew. Standing there in the bright light of day, I reminded myself that summer was coming at last; I could use the basket to carry cutlery out into the garden when friends came for lunch. Or I could go to France myself. Or to Italy. Or to Greece. I could install myself on my favorite Greek island. Already I could imagine the view down terraced hills to the Aegean. Already, sandals were perching in shoe store windows like brightly colored swallows.

And the long gray winter was almost over.

MARY GORDON
The Taste of Almonds

I am in Dublin having dinner with an Irish man of whom I am quite fond.

"Am I wrong in saying your family owned a sweet shop?" I ask him.

"Well, it was more than a sweet shop. It was a place that made all sorts of candies and some small cakes and what you call cookies; we would call them biscuits."

He has ordered profiteroles for dessert and I, abandoning my usual concern for calories, have joined him.

They are more wonderful than I could have hoped because the filling is not vanilla, but almond. Almond: my favorite flavor. The sweetness, which almost goes over the edge to excess, mixed with a hint of perfume, and a suggestion of health-giving protein, nutritive, a touch—maybe—of black earth. And perhaps a suspicion of the poisonous. Which is the poison that leaves a residual scent of almond? The one the clever detective is quick to pick up? Strychnine? Arsenic?

"May I tell you the subject of my first confession?" he asks.

"Of course," I say, hoping there will be no sudden revelations. I think we are both too old for sudden revelations. But there must be freedom of talk between us, because the evening has been a feast of talk, both of us apologizing for talking too much, each assuring the other, no, no, of course you haven't talked too much, you haven't talked enough. Go on. Please go on.

"What I confessed to in my first confession was that I had stolen a bar of almond paste. This was my first sin. I did lay down a couple of shillings for it. I was careful to tell the priest that; I thought maybe it would lessen the gravity."

I want to say to him: "Did you steal from your own father? Is it possible you didn't even have to steal? It's possible you had only to ask and he would have given it to you." But I don't know anything about his father. He may have been cruel. On the other hand, he may have been indulgent.

I am the child of an indulgent father, and one of his greatest indulgences is connected in my mind, not with the taste of almonds, but of pistachios.

I am three years old. I have just had my tonsils out and my throat is very very sore. The popular wisdom: ice cream must be given to children who have had their tonsils out. Ice cream is the thing that will both soothe and delight.

We live quite close to a Howard Johnson's, which boasts of offering thirty-seven flavors of ice cream. We live on the second floor in an apartment above the living quarters of our landlords, a family of Italians, more properly Sicilians. Each day, I am made happy by the smells, most notably strong coffee, that travel to us from the room below. Sometimes the smell of roasting nuts. Because my mother is a polio victim and the stairs are many, it falls to my father to get the ice cream for my soothing and delight.

I don't remember what my father offered first; possibly the most expected, chocolate or vanilla. But he can't interest me in chocolate or vanilla. I adamantly refuse. He keeps going back to Howard Johnson's. I can hear him each time, walking down the stairs, closing the heavy back door, walking back up. I can track this movement by the sound of the change in his pocket. Growing louder or softer as he approaches or retreats.

My father offers flavor after flavor. Peach, Strawberry, Vanilla Fudge. Nothing tempts me. He makes many trips and my mother, who is not indulgent, grows impatient. She shouts. "Just pick any one. We have a freezer full of ice cream now. Don't make your father go out again."

But, no, my father says, he only wants me to be happy. He is confident that he will, eventually, make me happy. That he will find the right flavor in time. The one that will soothe and delight.

After how many trips does my father return with pistachio? And what makes me know, immediately, that pistachio is the one? Is it the lovely green color? The alternation of light green and points of darkness: the actual nuts? I don't remember. I remember that the taste was exciting, with the particular excitement that accompanies a sense of rightness. Of precise belonging. "This is for me. This is mine."

But my mother introduces a note of anxiety. "What kind of a kid goes for pistachio?"

And I am reminded of the burdensome knowledge that I am not like other children, that I am constantly failing to fit the comfortable model of the ordinary child. Who would have been happy with chocolate or vanilla. Who might have thought to ask for strawberry, and been satisfied with that.

But I can hear in my mother's voice that she is secretly proud of the originality of my choice. Of its unpredictability. Sometimes when she praises me (not often), she says I have "a good imagination."

My father is entirely happy and proud. Proud that he has pleased me. Proud of his trips in and out of the house, up and down the stairs. Proud that he has relieved my pain.

For once, the three of us are happy. At the same time. For the same thing.

Last summer, in Sicily, I sat in an almond grove and drank cold white wine and ate roasted almonds, almonds from the very grove in which I sat.

I was staying in an *agroturismo,* an eighteenth-century farmhouse with not only almond but also olive trees, and a view of the sea and the ruins of Greek temples. Our host was a woman who had grown up in the house; her family had lived there for a century and a half. She had been an architect, working in Palermo. I see from photographs that she was a *jeune fille bien élevée;* she tells about her French schools and her English governess to explain how she is comfortable addressing us, Americans, and guests from the north of France. On the walls of our bedroom are charming drawings made by her mother in the thirties: madcap Flappers dropping crockery or being pulled by the jeweled leashes of their unruly miniature dogs.

Our host tells me how she came to be running an agroturismo. She perceived that unless she did something, the house would be lost: to decay or developers. She quit her job as an architect and studied organic farming, rescuing the old olive and, especially, the almond groves. Now she makes her living and ensures the safety of the property by taking in guests and selling products made of olive and almond.

I buy a bar of almond-scented soap. I can see that she is a happy woman. I admire her greatly. She saw reality and that the demands of reality required that she change her life. She changed her life, imaginatively, courageously, when she was no longer young. I am happy listening to her story as we eat and drink what she has brought into the world.

Once I read—or could I have heard it—a description of a woman's body as a peeled white almond. This was meant as praise. I have never had a body anything like a peeled white almond. I can no longer even remember why I once thought having a body like a peeled white almond was an enviable state. I remember, though, that I once did.

At the Dublin table next to my friend and me is a stunning girl. Her blond hair is piled high on her head and stiffly lacquered. Her eyes are heavily outlined in black. Her white silk shirt simultaneously emanates and absorbs light. At her throat is a single jewel: a diamond. Her fashionably grizzled boyfriend is on his iPhone a great deal of the time. They hardly speak to one another. She is eating a salad. In a small dish next to the salad is a little dressing. Occasionally, she dips the back of her fork into the dressing and applies it to a leaf of lettuce, which she eats slowly, carefully, chewing it many times. Occasionally, she takes a drink of sparkling water.

She will never order the profiteroles.

I will never be that stunning girl.

I am no longer young.

I close my eyes, soothed and delighted by the taste of almonds.

Some Pages from THE STORY OF MY HAND
L.K. Hanson

Let's talk hand lettering.

LAST YEAR, AFTER 30 YEARS WORKING AS A NEWSPAPER ARTIST, I WAS HIRED TO TEACH A COURSE IN HAND LETTERING AT AN ART SCHOOL IN ST. PAUL. MY TWENTYSOMETHING STUDENTS SHOWED UP FOR CLASS ARMED WITH MACBOOKS AND iPADS, KINDLES, AND ANDROIDS. I SHOWED UP WITH A BAG OF PENS, INKS, AND WRITING PAPER.

Can we use laptops for this class?

I WANTED THEM TO WRITE BY HAND, OFF THE KEYBOARD. I ASKED THEM TO WRITE AND DRAW "THE STORY OF MY HAND," MEANING THE HISTORY OF THEIR HANDWRITING. I DID A VERSION OF THE ASSIGNMENT WITH THEM.

WE TALKED ABOUT OUR LIVES AS ARTISTS, ABOUT THE CONCEPT OF "MAKING A MARK," THE SIGNIFICANCE OF LEAVING A REMINDER THAT "I WAS HERE." WE DISCUSSED THE LINK BETWEEN DRAWING AND WRITING, AND HOW ONE EVOLVED INTO THE OTHER. I SHOWED THE STUDENTS THE CAVE DRAWINGS FROM PECH MERLE IN FRANCE, EXQUISITE STENCILED HANDPRINTS MADE 25,000 YEARS AGO. ARTISTS LEAVING THEIR MARK.

OK, now tell me again what a fountain pen is.

71

Making Marks

My Mom   Aunt Esther

I started making my own mark early, drawing before I went to kindergarten. My earliest memory—and of beauty, I think—is the handwriting of my mother and her sisters, especially my Aunt Esther. They all learned their clear, legible hand in Iowa country schools. For these farm women, writing—good handwriting—was part of daily life in their homes. Examples were everywhere: letters and cards, recipes, notes, lists. I looked at these things and knew I wanted to do that—to write beautifully.

Mrs. Buck

I could write my name before first grade; that was all. Then, guided by Mrs. Buck, our kindly first grade teacher, it was time to learn to print.

Ee Ff
Rr Ss Tt

We practiced our block letters with No 2 Venus Velvet pencils, touching and lifting them over sheets of cheap lined paper, tiny splinters of wood snagging our pencils. We bore down and formed capitals and small letters, like the ones hanging above the blackboard.

Me, First Grade

I liked doing this, and I was good at it, good enough to be the class "good printer," the first step toward the "class artist" designation I gained in later years.

VENUS VELVET No 2   U.S.A.

THE BUNNY INCIDENT

IN THE SPRING OF THAT YEAR, IN A COMBO OF DO-GOODERISM AND RAW ARTISTIC HUBRIS, I DECIDED TO CREATE HANDMADE EASTER CARDS FOR MY CLASS. I MADE A BUNNY STENCIL, AND THEN CONSTRUCTION PAPER CUTOUTS. THEN, IN MY PERFECT BLOCK LETTERS, I PRINTED ON EACH CARD: "THIS RABITT WISHES YOU A HAPPY EASTER."

The evil Debbie Henderson

Dear Ben, This Rabitt wishes you a HAPPY EASTER — Larry H.

I PASSED OUT MY CARDS AND SAT DOWN, AWAITING THE HEAPS OF PRAISE I'D EARNED. DEBBIE HENDERSON, A SMART, SNOTTY FARM GIRL, RAISED HER HAND. "MRS. BUCK," SHE CHIRPED IN HER HIGH, SMARTY-PANTS VOICE, "HE SPELLED RABBIT **WRONG**."

THE WORD WAS MISSPELLED ON EVERY CARD.

PUBLIC HUMILIATION AT AGE SEVEN—UNDONE BY A TYPO (AND NOT FOR THE LAST TIME).

I LEARNED TO WRITE IN LONGHAND (THAT LOVELY OLD-FASHIONED TERM) IN THIRD GRADE. IT WAS HERE, TOO, THAT FOUNTAIN PENS ENTERED MY CONSCIOUSNESS: MRS. LUDVIG, OUR TEACHER, HAD ONE. I WATCHED—OK, STARED AT—MRS. LUDVIG AT HER DESK, HER PEN IN HER SLENDER FINGERS, GLIDING-STOPPING-GLIDING OVER A LESSON PLAN OR REPORT, HER HAND ENGAGED IN AN ELEGANT LITTLE BALLET THAT LEFT ME SPELLBOUND. HOW COULD I DO THAT?

Mrs. Ludvig

WE LEARNED WRITING USING THE UBIQUITOUS PALMER METHOD, A SYSTEM DEVELOPED IN THE LATE 19TH CENTURY. THE PALMER METHOD EMPHASIZED MAKING LEGIBLE AND EFFICIENTLY JOINED LETTERS. PERFECT PALMER EXAMPLES, LIKE OUR BLOCK LETTERS TWO GRADES EARLIER, HUNG ABOVE THE BLACKBOARD.

Palmer Method Letters

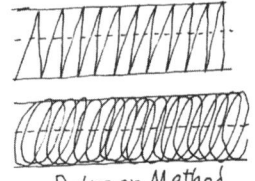
Palmer Method Practice

USING OUR Nº 2 VENUS VELVETS ON THE CHEAP LINED PAPER, WE MADE ENDLESS ROWS OF ZIG-ZAGS AND SMOKE RINGS. WE WERE DEVELOPING, MRS. L. SAID, **RHYTHM** IN OUR ARMS AND SHOULDERS, **RHYTHM** WHICH WOULD, IN TURN, MAKE US CAPABLE OF PERFECT, UNIFORM LETTERS.

I WORKED AT THIS. I LOVED MAKING SMOKE RINGS, THE FEEL OF THE PENCIL MOVING OVER THE PAPER. THIS SENSE OF HAVING AN EXTENSION OF MY HAND, AN EXTENSION ENABLING ME TO MAKE SOMETHING NEW AND BEAUTIFUL—THIS WAS THRILLING.

Larry Hanson
Lake Mills Ia
My hand c. 1954

NORA PALMER WAS MY FOURTH GRADE TEACHER. SHE WAS KIND, WARM, AND— NO SURPRISE—A DAZZLING MISTRESS OF THE FOUNTAIN PEN. I STILL HAVE, IN A LITTLE AUTOGRAPH BOOK I GOT IN 1953, AN ENDURING EXAMPLE OF HER BEAUTIFUL HAND:

Dear Larry, I have enjoyed being your teacher this year. May your life be like a snowflake, It leaves a mark but not a stain. With Love, Nora Palmer

Nora Palmer
1904-1982

THE LETTERS, IN BLUE FOUNTAIN PEN INK, ARE PERFECT. THE LINES REST PERFECTLY ON THE PAGE, AN EXQUISITE EXAMPLE OF A FINE HAND.

BECAUSE OF HER HANDWRITING, AND BECAUSE HER NAME WAS PALMER, I KNEW THAT MRS. PALMER—MY MRS. PALMER—WAS THE IN- VENTOR OF THE PALMER METHOD OF HANDWRIT- ING. HOW COULD SHE NOT BE? PROUDLY, I REPORT- ED THIS FACT TO ALL WHO WOULD LISTEN, UNTIL I LEARNED, PROBABLY FROM MRS. PALMER HERSELF, THAT I'D PERPETRATED A LIE. I STOOD CORRECTED, BUT UNWAVERING IN MY ADORATION OF MRS. PALMER.

A.N. Palmer
1860-1927
Inventor of the Palmer Method

IN FOURTH GRADE I BOUGHT MY FIRST FOUNTAIN PEN, A SHEAFFER CARTRIDGE, MADE IN FORT MADISON, IOWA, I WAS PROUD TO SAY. I MADE THIS PURCHASE AT NERBY'S DRUG IN LAKE MILLS. $1.49, INCLUDING A BONUS BOX OF FIVE CARTRIDGES.

THE DOWNSIDE OF A CARTRIDGE PEN, ESPECIALLY FOR AN UNEMPLOYED FOURTH GRADER WITH A 25¢ WEEKLY ALLOWANCE, WAS KEEPING IT IN CARTRIDGES. I CAME UP WITH A METHOD TO FILL USED CARTRIDGES, MUCH TO THE CONSTERNATION, I IMAGINED, OF THE GREEDY PEN PURVEYORS IN FORT MADISON: I BOUGHT A BOTTLE OF SHEAFFER'S SKRIP WRITING FLUID—NOT "INK," "WRITING FLUID"—AND A DRUG STORE EYEDROPPER, SECRETLY FILLING MY CARTRIDGES IN MY ROOM, ALWAYS WITH THE LOOMING SENSE THAT I WAS DOING SOMETHING ILLEGAL AND COULD BE BUSTED BY SHEAFFER GOONS AT ANY MOMENT.

My cartridge refill kit

MY SHEAFFER PEN WAS THE FIRST THING I REMEMBER HAVING THAT WAS AN **IMPORTANT** THING TO OWN. I KEPT IT WITH ME ALL THE TIME, IN MY SHIRT OR PANTS POCKET. IT RESTED ON MY DESK IN CLASS, AND ON MY DESK AT HOME; I ALWAYS KNEW WHERE IT WAS.

DEVELOPING A HAND

MY BEST FRIEND FROM FIFTH GRADE, AND UNTIL WE GRADUATED HIGH SCHOOL, WAS A BOY NAMED DAVID ROSHEIM. ROSHEIM (NEVER FIRST NAMES; TOO INTIMATE) LIVED IN TOWN WITH HIS GRANDPARENTS. HE WAS A SMART, GEEKY FOUR-EYES INTERESTED IN BOOKS, SCIENCE— AND FOUNTAIN PENS.

Me, c. 1955 *Rosheim, c. 1955*

ROSHEIM'S SCRAWLY, ILLEGIBLE HANDWRITING WAS ALREADY LEGENDARY IN FIFTH GRADE. BUT HE POSSESSED A **PARKER** FOUNTAIN PEN, A FANCY, REFINED GIFT FROM HIS COLLEGE-EDUCATED GRANDPARENTS. THIS ELEGANT INSTRUMENT MADE MY SHEAFFER LOOK LIKE A HOLLOW PLASTIC STICK WITH A TUBE OF INK STUCK IN IT (WHICH IT WAS).

Mrs. Palmer, with Rosheim's handwriting

"DAVID, I HAVE NO IDEA WHAT THIS SAYS."

I DEVELOPED SERIOUS PEN ENVY. CONSEQUENTLY, DRIVEN BY DESIRE, AND AT ROSHEIM'S URGING, I DECIDED AN UPGRADE WAS NECESSARY.

WHENEVER WE COULD, ROSHEIM AND I HUNG OUT AT STENSRUD'S DRUG STORE, A CHAOS OF WOODEN FLOORS, NARROW AISLES AND HIGH SHELVES CRAMMED WITH JARS, BOTTLES, BOXES, AND GOD KNOWS WHAT-ALL, OVERSEEN BY TINY BLANCHE STENSRUD, THE PROPRIETOR. ROSHEIM AND I PARKED OURSELVES AT THE MAGAZINE RACK TO GOSSIP, BEMOAN THE HELLISHNESS OF OUR SMALL TOWN LIVES, AND LOOK AT PEN ADS IN THE BIG, GLOSSY PAGES OF THE **SATURDAY EVENING POST** AND **LIFE**.

"BOYS, THIS ISN'T A LIBRARY, YOU KNOW."

STANDING AMIDST STENSRUD'S JUMBLE WAS A GLISTENING DISPLAY CASE, WHERE A COLLECTION OF PARKER PENS RESTED IN A GLASS-ENCASED UNIVERSE OF SOFT LIGHT AND SATIN-LINED GIFT BOXES. THIS IS WHERE I BOUGHT MY FIRST "GOOD" FOUNTAIN PEN, A PARKER "21". FIVE DOLLARS. BLACK PLASTIC. A SILVER CAP. THE TRADEMARK "ARROW" CLIP.

"WOW! THIS NEW SHEAFFER IS REALLY NEAT!"

Blanche Stensrud

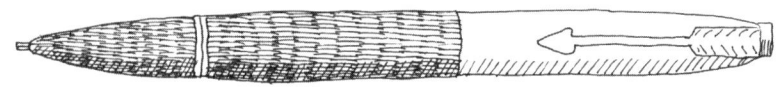

The Steinberg of Iowa

"WOW! WHAT'S THIS?"

In the early '60s I discovered the work of SAUL STEINBERG, the legendary **NEW YORKER** magazine artist. This happened at the heavy oak table next to the periodical rack at the Lake Mills public library, one of my high-school hangouts.

I'd never encountered anything like Steinberg's work. How did he DO this? How did he make drawing and writing work TOGETHER this way? All those thick and thin lines, the baroque curlicues, the splats and splatters. How did he **DO** that?

My version of Steinbergian lines

FOREST CITY • LAKE MILLS
IOWA

Answers were needed. What better way to find them than to imitate the man, to become my own Steinberg.

That summer, I stayed for a time with my grandparents in Forest City, a town not far from Lake Mills. Forest City was bigger than our town. It had a college. It had more stores. One was an all-purpose craft and hobby shop that

NOTE SIMILAR BLACK-FRAME GLASSES!

STEINBERG
Romanian Jew, lives in New York

HANSON
Scandinavian-Lutheran, lives on Iowa farm

77

Sold stuff like needlepoint supplies, model car and airplane kits, and art materials.

Here I got my Steinberg starter kit: a pen holder with a cork grip; some Hunt's Flexible Steel Nibs; and a bottle of Sanford's Penit Dubonnet (so French! so arty!) ink.

Hunt's Flexible Steel Nibs

"Koh-I-Noor" Pen Holder with cork grip

I practiced at my Grandma's oil-cloth covered kitchen table. Being completely on my own, I had no idea what I was doing. The god-awful pen was impossible: the nib snagged on the paper, leaving huge blobs and spatters, even holes. My cheap dime store "typing" paper didn't help, either — it sucked up ink like Kleenex and then crinkled like corrugated cardboard.

"WHAT TH...!!?"

I persisted, learning that a steel nib was all about pressure and control, and that a hard, smooth-surfaced paper was absolutely necessary for successful results.

Sanford's Penit Dubonnet Ink in fake cut-glass bottle

Iowan Steinberg

I managed to become my own version of Steinberg.

CHINA EGYPT EUROPE Atlantic Ocean THE EAST COAST IOWA

My Parker wasn't fancy, but it was a grownup pen, superior to the dime store Bic and Papermate ballpoints my high school classmates used. It left my Sheaffer in the dust. I had a Parker pen, which I knew made me **better** somehow, setting me above this corn-fed hick world where I'd been unjustly planted.

I started college in the fall of 1962, liberated at last. I arrived on the St. Olaf campus with fear, anticipation, and my Parker "21". I took my class notes with this pen, always in spiral-bound unruled notebooks because, as everyone knew (or should have known, I believed), fountain pen writing always looks best on plain, unlined paper. For making my art, I drew and worked in sketchbooks with my Parker, a constant, reliable extension of my hand, a tool of expression for the artist and writer I was becoming.

St. Olaf College

A college notebook

My Ink-Stained Wretch Years

From 1978 to 2007 I toiled in the newsroom of the **Minneapolis Star Tribune**, a place where everyone was a deadline demon. I drew and I wrote. I learned to be quick on the draw and fast on my feet. It was paradise. I wrote and illustrated a piece on the newly opened Mall of America. I covered the State Fair, the Renaissance Fair, the Uptown Art Fair. I made maps, lots of maps.

I still have an ancient Parker "21". It might be the one I had in college fifty years ago; I'm not sure. Its barrel is cracked, its cap scratched and dinged up, but it writes like a dream.

I DREW GRAPHS, CHARTS, AND TABLES. I PLOTTED THE COURSE OF BLIZZARDS, THE PATHS OF TORNADOES. I DID A LOT. I LEARNED A LOT. I LOVED MY JOB.

When my students and I first walked into that classroom last year, the room became common ground. I was the messenger from a communications past, carrying a bag of pens and inks and paper. The students were beings from the future, backpacks stuffed with electronic devices, buds in their ears. We were travelers on parallel paths, moving in opposite directions through the history of mark-making.

I was surprised by their willingness to try old methods and tools. Even the initially resistant "I only work digitally" gang gave over to the "primitive" dip pen. As the class progressed, students moved deeper into the written past, seeking the history of letterforms, acquiring old-fashioned implements like fountain pens for themselves.

"HEY, LK! IS THE LAMY 2000 A GOOD PEN DEAL?"

Our classroom, a windowless basement with stone walls and a vaulted brick ceiling, was our scriptorium. That's how I'll always see my students: monastic scribes, perched on tall stools, hunkered over their desks. They're doing an assignment in pen and ink, the only sound being the "skritch-skritch" of steel nibs on paper. Except for the occasional "OH, SHIT!", I think they're enjoying themselves. They've come into my world.

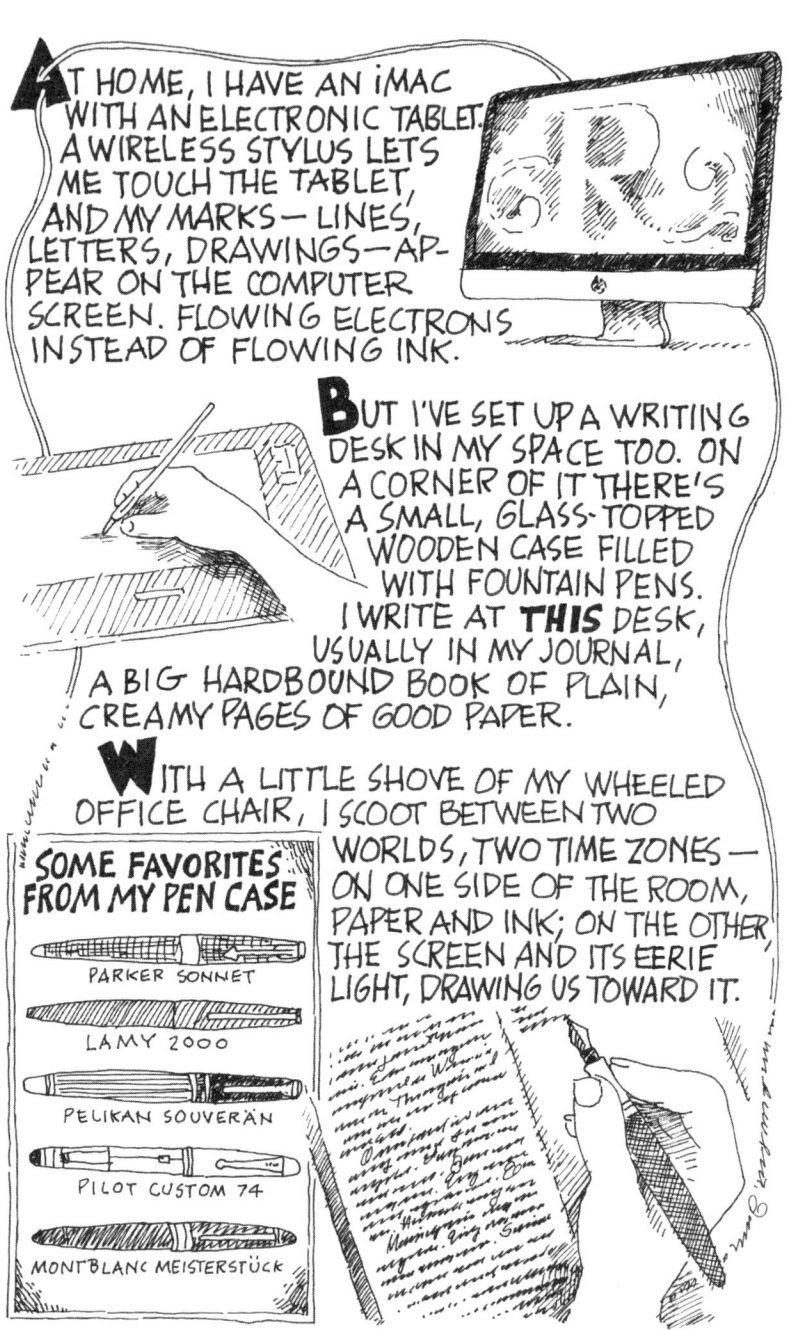

PHILLIP LOPATE
Why I Remain a Baseball Fan

I sometimes encounter ex–baseball fans (invariably middle-aged men) who tell me they have given up following the sport because of the steroid scandal, the huge salaries of the players, the duplicity of the owners—"It's all become just a big business," or some such explanation, which they deliver in a tone of principled disgust. I listen with feigned sympathy, but of course I don't share their feelings, either because I have many fewer principles or the ones I have lie in other directions, and I would not dream of relinquishing the pleasure (and pain) of a new baseball season. I anticipate being a baseball fan until I lose all my marbles, and possibly beyond that.

The fact is I have never been a particularly good athlete, and I can no more begrudge baseball superstars getting hundred-million-dollar contracts for doing what I could never do than I would resent well-paid Hollywood actors who manage to radiate aching beauty and charisma onscreen. I have noticed that most of the men who object to the so-called inflated salaries of ballplayers have larger bank accounts than my own. If they had grown up poor, as I did, they might not have figured it was any of their business to identify with and assess the remunerative levels of ballplayers, but simply assumed these demigods would always be incomparably above them.

I grew up in the 1940s in working-class Brooklyn. Both my parents were factory workers, and of course I rooted for the Brooklyn Dodgers, that storied team. My father took me to Ebbets Field for a Sunday doubleheader with St. Louis: the first game was a duel between the Cardinals ace and my favorite Dodger pitcher, Don Newcombe (I liked his big-jawed grin) that went to extra innings, 0-0, before Stan Musial hit a home run in the tenth. What a thrill to watch a great player like Musial connect, even if he was on the opposing team. Most of all I liked to watch Jackie Robinson dancing off third base, taunting the pitcher. Robinson, Carl Furillo, Roy Campanella, Gil Hodges, Duke Snider, et al., are often celebrated as the archetypal "lunch pail" ballplayers, who lived in the neighborhood and rode the trolleys or subways to Ebbets Field. Supposedly, they were "like us," a nice fairy tale, but in the neighborhood, we viewed them as superheroes, not blue-collar workers like our fathers. Besides, baseball players are not cops or civil servants: I see no reason why they should be expected to live within the city limits of the locality named on their uniforms. It's true that Ebbets Field had an intimacy—you felt as though you could touch the center fielder—but maybe that's why attendance and profits dropped off near the end. In any case, one good thing about rooting for the Dodgers was that when their owner, Walter O'Malley, broke our hearts by moving the team out to Los Angeles in 1958, for the most logically mercenary of reasons, I lost my innocence in one fell swoop and never had to be quite as shocked, surprised, or appalled again.

In a sense, the Dodgers' move away from us was anticlimactic because they had already won their first World Series, which was what mainly counted to me as a kid. It was such an important event that the principal of our public school allowed the final innings of the last game to be broadcast over the P.A. system. So the Dodgers triumphed, they were no longer losers, Dem Bums, and were free to go off to sunny California. For a while I rooted for the Los Angeles Dodgers, unable to stop caring about Sandy Koufax and Don Drysdale (whom I cheered on during their salary sit-down strike), John Roseboro, and Junior Gilliam. But then when the New York Mets got started, I switched allegiance to them, as did millions of other ex–Dodger fans. Part of the reason was geographical: the Mets played in Queens, which was adjacent to Brooklyn (the same long island). Sure, we had the option to turn into Yankee fans, but we didn't: the Yankees were associated in our minds with the G.O.P. and Big Business, the Dodgers (the first team to integrate racially) with liberalism and labor. I now consider such characterizations nonsense, since all baseball teams are millionaires' playthings. In the seventies, when the Mets were about to trade Tom Seaver to the Reds for a bunch of mediocre players, I called the front office and begged them not to do it. I registered my displeasure, as did many other Mets fans, but was not at all surprised that our protests were ignored: I had already become inured, courtesy of Walter

O'Malley, to owner shenanigans, having learned once and for all that baseball is indeed a business. And so, let the games begin.

It is sometimes posited as an enigma that anyone can continue to root for the same team after its star players have been traded away, or after the players themselves have allegedly betrayed their loyal fans by signing for more money elsewhere as free agents—in other words, after the roster has been completely reshaped. I find this no mystery: the cells in one's body are replaced every seven years, and yet one continues to retain the same individuality. One may continue to love one's country, in spite of its misbegotten wars and scurvy domestic policies. If consumers remain loyal to brands, and continue to buy Toyotas despite its corporate changes in design, why not a baseball team, which has a shared history, a tradition, and even a style of play? Some ballparks with deep outfield dimensions promote pitching; others, power hitters or base-stealers. The essence of a team's identity, its tendency to choke or rise to the occasion—its karma, if you will—is felt by its fans, however superstitious those expectations may be. The Cubs show promise at the beginning of the season and fade at the end. The Twins do better than anyone expected. The Mets, give or take a few illustrious seasons, are a .500 team, and the Yankees are champions, though both play in the same big-money market.

Part of becoming a grown-up is accepting one's limitations. As I said, I am not a good athlete, though my tennis game has lately improved; I am something of a klutz, but I have moments of surprising grace. So it is with my team. Becoming a baseball fan means learning to absorb failure and be on a friendly footing with defeat. Your team, considered as a whole, will not win year after year: if it gets to two World Series in a decade, it is doing phenomenally well. Every baseball fan knows this. When blowhard owners make speeches about there being no excuse for coming in second, because the only thing that counts is winning, the true fan yawns and takes this for gasconade. If, as Montaigne wrote, "To philosophize is to learn how to die," then to be a baseball fan is to learn how to lose. Ivan Morris once wrote a fine book called *The Nobility of Failure,* in which he argued that the heroic tradition in Japanese history and narrative culture was built around the general who fails, the samurai who, surrounded and outnumbered, falls on his sword. Perhaps it isn't surprising that the Japanese have taken to baseball.

I can still see in my mind's eye the Mets' former star outfielder Carlos Beltrán, with the tying run in scoring position and two men out and the count full, frozen by Adam Wainwright's curveball—the pitch that ended the Mets' season. I still ask myself: why can't Mets hitters learn to foul off more of those borderline pitches? Why are they so one-dimensional? And wasn't that pitch a little outside? A team's key defeats stay so much fresher in the mind—in my mind, at least—than do its victories. We tend to adjust easily to victory; we need little schooling in that department. Baseball teaches us bitter wisdom.

The older I get, the more fascinated I am watching the aging process in my favorite baseball players, their limps and lingering injuries, which point the way to my own diminished arthritic future. The Mets used to make a habit of signing aging sluggers, like George Foster, Eddie Murray, or Gary Carter, who would then demonstrate "warning track" power, no longer able to hit home runs but specializing in deep fly-ball outs. The look of dismay, almost shame, on the faces of these once-omnipotent power hitters (*vide* the Yankees' Jorge Posada or Alex Rodriguez) as they circle back to the dugout, having watched their ball land impotently in the outfielder's glove, is a lesson on the vanity of human endeavor. We are all dust in the wind.

Of course being a baseball fan is not all about accustoming oneself to decline: there are those remarkable debuts, like the rookie seasons of Ken Griffey, Jr., or Jose Reyes, when blazing young talents joyously revel in their speed and prowess; or the sophomore year of talented players who begin to put it all together. Part of the pleasure in baseball is matching expectation to outcome: the hard-working, nondescript-looking Dustin Pedroia accomplishes more than larger, more muscled players and wins the MVP award. A runt like the shortstop Bucky Dent, one of their least dangerous hitters, belts the home run that salvages the Yankee season. Those dramatic reversals of character, when adrenaline propels the shrimp to excel in postseason while the stud falls into an 0-for-20 swoon, are like a passage out of Homer: the gods and goddesses have whimsically lent support to some minor figure on the field, infusing him with their celestial spirit, while abandoning their usual darling.

Here we come to the most essential reason I cling to baseball: its ability to generate narrative. The baseball season is like a long, complicated, drama series on television—*The Wire*, *The Sopranos*, or *Mad Men*—where you follow various quirky characters and become invested in their fates. That the craven yes-man should act in an atypically bold manner, or the cold-blooded killer suddenly show prudence, remains a key part of such television series' appeal. I would not expect a viewer to come upon an episode of *The Wire* in the middle of the second season and make sense of what was happening, any more than I would expect my wife to know baseball when she idly watches a game behind me for five minutes without knowing the players and their past histories or potentials. I fully appreciate why she finds the mere spectacle of baseball insufficient. Without knowing the individual players as a cast of characters, it is a pretty dull, abstract ballet. But once they are known, then every at-bat turns into a short story, with the pitcher moving the ball around, trying to hit his spots, and the batter trying to second-guess what's coming next. And if you know, in addition, that the new relief pitcher just arrived the day before from the minor leagues because another relief pitcher was injured, and he is facing Albert Pujols, perhaps the most fearsome hitter in baseball, the David-and-Goliath narrative wheels start turning automatically.

Then there is the dynastic dimension—the father-and-son duos that made it to the big leagues, or the many sets of brothers who play against each other for different teams. There are the baseball scouts who traditionally sign up players of a certain skill-set, or from a specific group of colleges, or from a particular Dominican or Puerto Rican town. All of this intriguing if petty historical knowledge, which probably takes a lifetime of following baseball to acquire, makes baseball seem like a small southern town where everyone knows everyone's kin. Dave Magadan is Lou Piniella's godson, that kind of thing. It adds to the game's novelistic texture.

Baseball has always attracted serious writers, a mixed blessing. I am not one of those authors tempted to gush about the April zephyrs lifting opening day banners, the verdant velvet swards, the elegant geometry of the bases…Yeah, we know, baseball has a poetic side, but it's been overemphasized. I did not remain a lifelong baseball fan because of the smell of peanuts and hot dogs. I mostly watch it on television, so that sensual aspect is beside the point: the color of the grass merely the best green my HD TV can yield at any one moment. I watch for the storyline: what's going to happen next.

With such powerful inducement to keep me engaged, perhaps you understand why I was not put off baseball forever by learning that some of the players doped themselves with steroids. Yes, it was unfortunate, and tarnished in our minds many records broken at the height of steroid use. But I view it as one more impurity to accept in this life. The old ballplayers drank; my childhood idol Don Newcombe was often stewed on the days he pitched. Dock Ellis pitched a no-hitter on acid. Granted, alcohol and LSD offer fewer physical advantages than steroids. But I still think it took incredible hand-eye coordination and skill to hit homers the way Barry Bonds did. For every Barry Bonds or Sammy Sosa or Rafael Palmeiro, who went from being all-stars to superstars with the aid of steroids, there were dozens of journeymen who shot themselves with juice constantly but didn't improve much. Look, I am glad steroid use is monitored and has abated; but I wouldn't be surprised if some other advantageous substance or sneaky technology were employed in the future. Baseball players are always looking for an edge, be it pine tar or spy cameras; it is part of the evolution of the game.

Nor do I buy the idea that baseball players must behave like role models for youth and therefore shouldn't drink, gamble, or fornicate. Sports media today rarely offer illuminating insights into the way a game is actually played; but they are filled with stories of ballplayers' misdeeds off-field. Every sports columnist sets up as a pontificating Savonarola. Baseball players, whether active or retired, are indeed sinners like the rest of us; and out of curiosity I am as happy as the next man to read about their barroom brawls, speeding tickets, misadventures holing up with strippers, or being caught with illegal drugs; their committing of suicide, murder, rape, statutory rape, negligent homicide while driving; their filing for bankruptcy, embezzling, and shoplifting; their beating girlfriends, being stabbed by girlfriends, swapping wives, getting run in by the local police for lying naked and asleep with a prostitute in a car on Main Street, Florida, during exhibition baseball season, and so on and so forth. But what has any of this got to do with the itch to turn on a ballgame on a summer night?

I have no idea how the peccadilloes or felonies of baseball players statistically compare with a similar population sampling. We rarely hear the other side of the story—how some ballplayer put his child to bed or helped his wife through a difficult situation with her parents. Not that I would want the sports pages to be clogged with such goody-goody anecdotes either. The point I am making is that all of these peeks into the private lives and moral frailties of players (or owners, whose messy divorces and susceptibility to Ponzi schemes have become headline fodder of late—wait, even the longtime clubhouse manager of the Mets was recently arrested for stealing equipment and uniforms) have no bearing whatsoever on why I remain a loyal baseball fan. There is virtually nothing the players or owners or batboys can do that can disillusion me to the point of alienating me from the sport. It's a game that I simply like to follow, pitch by pitch. As long as they play, I will watch.

NANCY LORD
My Acid Cruise

I thought I'd grow up to be a scientist. As a child I was infatuated with pet mice and guppies and studying trees from the shapes of their leaves. And don't I remember, as a kindergartner, being ushered into the school basement to watch on TV the Russian satellite, Sputnik, soaring into outer space? We were lectured on the spot to start studying science and math, or the Russians would pound us all into the ground.

There was no higher goal than to reach for the stars or dive to the bottom of the sea, to comprehend the universe. The Alan Shepards and Jacques Cousteaus who did these things were our heroes. King science and its applied technology informed our lives and the promise that was the future. Who knew, in that bright and shining time, that so much in our culture and politics would soon turn corrosive?

But along the way, I found that science—the actual *doing* of it—is tedious, at least compared with watching guppies eat their young. The collection of data is a repetitive business, the same careful measurements over and over, across hours and days, years, decades. You gain small increments of understanding—or perhaps not. Your only understanding may be one of failure: an inability to find pattern or meaning, the need for more data, additional data sets, a new theory.

We don't have time for this. We're an impatient people. I'm speaking of Americans now. We don't trust science, in any case. We don't understand it, which is reason enough not to trust it or the people in the white coats who, surely, can manipulate numbers any way they want as part of that vast scientific conspiracy to get rich off government funding.

Why spend tax dollars for a bunch of wonky people to measure cow farts or fuss over some bit of whatever floating around in the ocean? We know what we know, anyway. We don't need those fancy-pants, with their heads in clouds and all those crazy charts and numbers, to tell us how to live.

But wait. We don't understand irony either.

*

Instead of a scientist, I became a writer of the creative sort, but then—wouldn't you know?—the fish and the trees and the stars all kept calling to me and, increasingly, seemed to demand attention for more than their own sakes. In a crowded, warming world, I was drawn back both to the wonders of nature and to wanting to better understand the systems we all rely on.

And so I find myself, the lone writer among scientists, aboard the research vessel *Tiglax,* on Alaska's Seward Line. September along the southern coast is often stormy—not an ideal time to boat on the open ocean. But here I am.

The Seward Line: an imaginary straight line that extends from the mouth of Resurrection Bay south of Seward, Alaska, 150 miles into the Gulf of Alaska, to where the continental shelf falls off into very deep water. The Seward Line: also the name of a long-term observation program that studies changes in the marine system, especially in relationship to climate variability. There are twenty-two stations spaced along the Line, and we—a team from the University of Alaska Fairbanks, made up mostly of volunteer graduate students, with a couple of professors and me, a writer invited to help bring some public awareness to the work—stop at each station to collect basic oceanographic data. When we finish, we duck into Prince William Sound and do the same at stations there.

We are enormously lucky on this week-long cruise. The sea has been so calm that the other day we drifted with a pair of fin whales and could see, looking down through the glassy blue surface, the entire body length of the whales as they passed by and under us. The larger one, when it lined up beside us, approached our own 120-foot length. Pale chevron markings descended its dark back. Its white right jaw, distinct from its dark left one, flashed as it must flash when the whale uses it to herd prey fish into tight schools it can swallow in a gulp.

Toby Burke, a federal biologist assigned to the team for a bird count, complains good-naturedly about the calm. Other falls he's seen more birds when the weather whips up, when the pelagic species blow in toward shelter and nutrients stir up from below to provide more food for everything that needs to eat at and near the surface.

Now, having reached the far end of the Seward Line, we finally meet an open-ocean swell—nothing compared with more typical seas that other years have chased the ship back to Resurrection Bay. On the flying bridge, Toby counts out northern fulmars, shearwaters, black-footed albatrosses with their long, scythed wings. The birds appear singly, out of the distance, flapping through the still air instead of gliding on a wind. Something else—thick-bodied, gray as a gull, a bird I've never even *heard* of, a south polar skua. "South polar" because it breeds all the way down on the Antarctic coast; then, during the austral winter, it migrates thousands of miles to the North Pacific to steal food from other birds. As we watch, it swoops after a shearwater, driving it down to the water, where the lesser bird presumably coughs up its meal.

The birds leave us, and I study the watery horizon all the way around. Sky and sea, blue and bluer, the slightest curve suggesting the ball that is Earth. Nothing else in sight—nothing except, like a pinpoint in space, this toy boat bobbing. This, I think, is what *oceanic* means: vastness dwarfing all that is human, our self-importance, our self-assigned centrality. Birds could live a lifetime here and never have a set of binoculars aimed at them. This is the world as it must have looked at the dawn of time, when our ancestors crawled from the sea.

Despite its expanse—wide and deep and all around—and despite my romantic sense of the ocean as fixed and forever, immutable, we now know that the ocean—everything in nature—changes with time. There is no perfect equilibrium. The North Pacific Ocean today is not identical to the one that existed a billion years ago or a thousand or hundred years ago or even last year.

In just the four decades of my Alaska residence, this ocean climate has shifted from one favoring benthic species like crab and shrimp to one more favorable to pollock and other finned fish. The 1989 *Exxon Valdez* oil disaster painted the shoreline behind us with toxic sludge, after which Prince William Sound's herring sickened and disappeared. Also among the disappeared are most members of what had been a well-known killer whale pod. And Toby has told me that he counts only a fraction of those birds surveyed in the 1970s and 1980s. Common murres—the penguinesque seabirds that nest colonially on cliffs and dive after fish and invertebrates—are especially diminished.

Change, yes.

That's why we're here. Not specifically to study fish or whales or even birds, but to collect basic oceanographic data—physical, chemical, and biological—that will help with understanding seasonal cycles and variability from year to year. In spring, with the light and warmer temperatures and fueled by the all-important nutrients that stir up from deeper water during the winter, plankton grow rapidly and dramatically in what are called blooms—or what the scientists call *primary production*. Now, in September, we're again measuring temperature, salinity, pH, nutrients, and the last pulse of plankton, numbers and kinds of zooplankton (animals) that have eaten the phytoplankton (plants). The zooplankton have fed the fish and the birds, the whales. They all link together—the salmon that so many Alaskan families depend upon to the zooplankton, to the phytoplankton, to the conditions that benefit, or not, the primary production. I don't need to be a scientist to understand that everything's related; everything here connects.

On the back deck of the *Tiglax* our crew hauls aboard the CTD, a $150,000 scientific instrument tethered to an armored communications cable. It measures conductivity (salinity), temperature, and depth (pressure). It's also called a rosette, for the carousel of twelve bottles that are "fired" at different depths for water sampling.

I pull up my overturned bucket and take my place with two grad students, Kristin Shake and Amy Rathe, to decant those canisters into a variety of other bottles. Kristin takes her samples first, before any air mixes with the water; these will be tested later for their alkalinity and dissolved inorganic carbon.

Amy and I follow along, the three of us knee to knee, sliding our seat-buckets as we circle the CTD. This sampling is like nothing so much as milking a cow. Each canister has a nipple to grab and tug, to make the water flow, and we sit like milkmaids around our beast. We rinse each bottle three times, fill to the appropriate level, rinse the cap,

cap, and set the bottle back in the milk crate. Move to the next canister. Uncap, rinse, rinse, rinse, fill, cap.

This is monkeywork, tedious, repetitive, exactly what I'd chosen to avoid in eschewing a career in science. I'm at last learning what it is to be a scientist, or at least what it's like to be a science student. I'm impressed with our crew of volunteers, not a slacker among them. If they need to be on deck at daybreak, they're out there in full gear before the sky lightens, kidding around, helping one another with whatever needs to be done. They solve every mechanical and practical problem that comes along and are exacting with every measurement and task. Their enthusiasm is contagious, their intellectual curiosity reassuring to our collective future.

I'm working without gloves, and the water, coming from two thousand meters below, is icy-cold, close to freezing. The surface water, meanwhile, is surprisingly warm, not yet mixed with deeper water by fall storms. At fifty-five degrees Fahrenheit, it about matches the air temperature.

Chase Stoudt, who runs the casting and firing part of the operation—the computer-monitored lowering and raising of the CTD and the snapping shut of each bottle at its appropriate depth—tells me, "The CTD data from the stations are like a CAT scan of the brain. Repeat readings of the same data at the same locations show the change over time." Figuring out how to measure salinity electronically took forty years, he says. "The equivalent challenge to sending a man to the moon."

We haul our bottles into the lab where we put some into the freezer and pour others, labeled *totals* and *fractals,* through filters that collect their chlorophyll—the pigment plants use to capture the sun's energy. We label, store, prepare for the next cast. Kristin's glass bottles go into red plastic totes; she'll have some six hundred samples to take back to the university lab. There, she and other lab assistants will spend days and weeks, months, sending the samples through an analytical instrument. (Later, when I visit this machine in Fairbanks, its snake nest of tubes will look like something from Dr. Jekyll's fiendish lab.)

Dall's porpoises are shooting around the stern of the ship, their quick cuts through the surface throwing up rooster tails of spray, the white trim to dorsals and tail flukes accenting their here-and-gone torpedo shapes.

Toby's bird count is up to thirty-six species, including a Laysan albatross and, of all things, a horned lark that must have been on a long migration across the gulf.

It's established that in the past couple of centuries, human activities, including deforestation and the burning of fossil fuels, have significantly increased the carbon dioxide in the atmosphere, where it acts as a greenhouse gas to trap heat. This global warming has resulted in changes to the global climate. The American public, however, remains either confused or unconcerned and sometimes combative about this research-based data. In a 2011 national survey by the Yale Project on Climate Change Communication, published as "Climate Change in the American Mind," 63 percent of respondents agreed that global warming is happening, but only 50 percent said they believed it is caused mostly by human activities. Thirty-nine percent believed "there is a lot of disagreement among scientists about whether global warming is happening." Only 6 percent considered the issue of global warming to be "extremely important" to them personally, while 15 percent said it was "not at all important" personally.

In a similar Yale survey a year earlier ("Americans' Knowledge of Climate Change"), 77 percent of those polled said they'd never heard of ocean acidification, the newish (since 2003) term that references the chemical change in the ocean due to increased carbon dioxide absorption. OA, as it's also known, is "the other CO_2 problem" or, more ominously, "global warming's evil twin." While the study of OA is still in its infancy, some scientists theorize that the effects of OA on ocean ecosystems and world food production will be more devastating than those of global warming.

Just as everything in the ocean connects, so do the ocean and the atmosphere couple into an integrated system that exchanges heat, water, and gases. Of all the carbon dioxide that human activities have released to the atmosphere, about a third has been absorbed into the ocean. This ocean "buffering" for a long time was thought to be a good thing—something to help ease global warming. Some scientists actively tried to figure out how to force more atmospheric carbon dioxide across the interface.

But now we know: that huge new contribution of carbon dioxide into the ocean has changed the ocean's chemistry. The ocean is becoming more acidic, less alkaline. It is now 30 percent more acidic than it was two hundred years ago, and projections are that by the end of this century the increase in acidity may be 200 percent. Such large changes—both in degree and rapidity—are thought not to have occurred for at least twenty-one million years. The marine ecosystems we enjoy today evolved over time in a stable pH environment, and their organisms tend to be very sensitive to ocean pH. How will they respond to this bitter new world?

The basic chemistry I'm coming to understand is this: carbon dioxide in the atmosphere remains carbon dioxide, with its bonded carbon and oxygen atoms. But it reacts with seawater to form carbonic acid, which releases hydrogen ions, thereby reducing pH. (Acidity or alkalinity of a solution is determined by the amount of hydrogen ions in it, with an ion being an atom with a charge.) Those hydrogen ions then combine with carbonate ions to form bicarbonate. This removes carbonate ions from the water, reducing the number available to make calcium carbonate, the major mineral building block of shell-builders. Those shell-builders include the obvious ones—corals, crabs, mussels, clams, snails, oysters, sea stars—but they also include many planktonic calcifiers at the base of the food chain, upon which so much else in the marine system depends. Their shell-building is made more difficult, and if and when carbonate concentrations fall too low, already formed calcium carbonate starts to dissolve.

Scientists have found that our cold northern waters—which can absorb more carbon dioxide than warmer waters—are already "undersaturated with respect to aragonite," one of the two principal forms of calcium carbonate. Undersaturation is expected in the deep ocean, below what is known as the "saturation horizon," but that horizon has been moving upward, essentially squeezing out the habitat supportive of shell-building. Our predecessors on the Seward Line and on other oceanographic cruises around the Alaskan coast have been shocked to find that the relatively shallow waters atop the continental shelf already

Subscribe to
PLOUGHSHARES

☐ Send me a one-year subscription for $30.
I save $12 off the cover price (3 issues).

☐ Send me a two-year subscription for $50.
I save $34 off the cover price (6 issues).
Unless you indicate otherwise, your subscription will begin with the Winter 2012-13 issue.

☐ This is a renewal

☐ Payment enclosed ☐ Bill me later

Name _____

Address _____

_____

E-mail address _____

Add $30 per year for international postage ($10 for Canada).
Subscribe or renew online: www.pshares.org.

Gift Subscriptions

☐ Send a one-year gift subscription for $30 to:
Friend _____
Address _____
_____
Gift Message _____

☐ Send a one-year gift subscription for $30 to:
Friend _____
Address _____
_____
Gift Message _____

☐ Payment enclosed ☐ Bill me later

Name _____

Address _____

_____

E-mail address _____

Your gift subscription will begin with the Fall 2012 issue, unless you indicate otherwise. We will mail a letter to announce your gift. Add $5.00 for Priority Mail for the first issue (domestic only). Add $30 per year for international postage ($10 for Canada). Subscribe or renew online: www.pshares.org.

BUSINESS REPLY MAIL
FIRST-CLASS MAIL   PERMIT NO. 2681   BOSTON, MA

POSTAGE WILL BE PAID BY ADDRESSEE

PLOUGHSHARES

EMERSON COLLEGE

120 BOYLSTON ST.

BOSTON, MA 02116-4624

BUSINESS REPLY MAIL
FIRST-CLASS MAIL   PERMIT NO. 2681   BOSTON, MA

POSTAGE WILL BE PAID BY ADDRESSEE

PLOUGHSHARES

EMERSON COLLEGE

120 BOYLSTON ST.

BOSTON, MA 02116-4624

have a pH low enough to be corrosive to shell-building. The data from our trip will help track that change over time, adding to the pattern of what is known and what might be expected.

That's the chemistry. Chemistry determines biology, and changes in the ocean's chemistry will influence the life forms that live in its waters.

Russ Hopcroft, chief scientist for our cruise, talks to me about what he calls Cinderella science. "It's science that's not appreciated but could turn into something beautiful," he says. "Long-term data sets are so important, but nobody wants to fund them. If publication is your goal, then this is not a productive way to do science. But if you want to measure change, you can't get it any other way."

In other words, the kind of monitoring done on the Seward Line, year after year, is unsexy.

Seward Line data collection, as a focused and systematic effort, began in 1998 as part of something called GLOBEC (Global Ocean Ecosystems Dynamics), an international program for examining the potential effect of global warming on ocean ecosystems. GLOBEC funding (from the National Science Foundation) ended in 2004, and a reduced program has since bumped along with patched-together grants (mostly from the North Pacific Research Board) and the hope that a new funding partnership will commit long-term to two cruises—spring and fall—each year.

"We need at least ten years to begin to see patterns," Russ—whose work is principally with zooplankton—says. "We don't know what the pH change will mean for animals. It may take many years to know how the ecosystem responds, and our monitoring will have to be accompanied by more controlled lab experiments." He pauses before adding, "Without knowing the background pattern, what we see in any year could just be random. The more observations—the more statistical value."

Russ shows me some charts on his computer: along the Seward Line for the past twelve years, water temperatures at the top of the water column. There were some very warm springs, and then, in the past couple of years, cooler ones. Now it's warmer again. In fall, there was less difference among years but greater difference between inshore waters and farther out, with warmer water trapped along the coast by currents. In general, warmer waters in both seasons correlated with increased growth rates of commercial species, like salmon—but only when there was enough food. "We're finding that things are more complicated than we originally thought," Russ says. "That's why we're here. We need to see the ocean as one big interrelated ecosystem."

He clicks to another set of charts, showing the prevalence of nutrients that fuel the phytoplankton that feed the zooplankton that feed the fish—the salmon and pollock that people care about. This is what Russ and his colleagues are trying to get to—information that will be of practical help to those who manage and participate in fisheries. They're trying to understand mechanisms and correlations, to demonstrate the real-life value of science. It's slow work. "We can't test hypotheses," he says, "like 'let's warm up the Gulf of Alaska and see what happens.' But we can patiently observe such changes when they 'naturally' occur. To do so we need the annual data sets."

He clicks again, to a set of photos, stunning shots of various zooplankton species in all their spiny, feathery, tubular, translucent beauty. This is his real passion, Russ says—taking these photos through microscopes. "People can find zooplankton interesting," he tells me. If they do, I fear, most people find them interesting not as microscopic creatures in a giant ocean but when they're brought into sight as exotic creatures that could be standing at a Star Wars bar. Later, I realize that many of the photo illustrations of zooplankton I've pored over in scientific journals, popular magazines, and on the Web are credited to Russ.

In the ship's dry lab, Russ oversees three students sorting through living zooplankton they collected with a fine-mesh net dropped over the side at our last station. It takes skill and fortitude to stare into a microscope at sea, and the sea has been cooperating. Each woman places a water sample in a shallow dish under her scope, then uses an eyedropper to suck up one tiny critter after another, identifying and counting each one.

The numbers of zooplankton captured in the nets are low compared with other years, Russ says—fewer than he expected but about the same composition in terms of species. The students are looking at lots of copepods—the dominant zooplankton members, with bullet-shaped bodies, long antennae, and the "oar feet" that give them their name.

Another project takes place at night, when zooplankton migrate upward to gather near the surface and feed. I stayed up for a previous night while the night crew towed a "Multinet," a contraption with five fine-meshed nets, each of which deploys at a different depth. In the dark, a half moon leapt all over the sky, and small silvery fish caught the light as they threw themselves, like popping corn, from the water at our stern. When the nets were back on board, the crew washed them down, concentrating their haul into cod-end canisters poured off into jars and fixed for analysis back at the university. The collections looked like slime soup, swarmy with the shrimplike euphausiids. One net held a couple of knuckle-length lanternfish, squished by the pressure in the net. Most fish can outswim the nets, and those that get caught, I was told, are sick, dying, or dead.

In the lab, Russ invites me to take a look through the scope at a pteropod, *Limacina helicina*. Pteropods ("winged feet") are essentially small swimming snails, with feet adapted to look and act like wings that help move them through the water. Magnified, they're pretty little animals, sometimes called sea angels or sea butterflies.

In the scope, the juvenile pteropod is a busy critter, spinning wildly around like a flipped-out insect. When it pauses I get a look at its "wings," fragile and trembling pale appendages. The shell part of it is less obvious to me. Grown up, this species can reach three-eighths of an inch in size, like a small brown lentil in a whirled shell.

"There are only two kinds here," Russ says. "The other one is bigger and much less common." The other one, *Clione limacina,* is known as a "naked" pteropod; that is, it has a shell as a newly hatched larva but soon casts it off to drift around unprotected.

These little animals, so unimposing in themselves, play a huge role in the marine food web, especially in high-latitude seas. They're eaten by other zooplankton, fish, whales, and marine birds. Juvenile salmon in particular depend on them; one study showed they made up 60 percent of a pink salmon's diet. That's now. The future may be very different. If pteropods' ability to build shells is compromised by increasing acidification, as controlled laboratory studies have demonstrated; the cascading effects through this marine ecosystem—and others at both ends of the world—will be profound. The pteropod is coming to be known as the "poster invertebrate" of ocean acidification, just as the polar bear is the poster child of climate change.

Jellyfish, among the largest members of the zooplankton community, drift around the ship, bells pulsing and tentacles waving. Most of them are smaller than dessert plates and nearly translucent, like pale reflections of the moon; in fact, the common *Aurelia* species are popularly known as moon jellies. A larger brown one—of the cold-water species called "lion's mane"—comes close to us, and Amy leans out with a net to scoop it onto the deck. The animal that was so beautifully globe-like and flowing in the water collapses into a brown, inert puddle. We gather around, hands away from the stinging tentacles, while Russ points out features, and then Amy drops it back into the sea.

"Jellies" are among the most ancient of sea creatures, going back perhaps five hundred million years. They're not actually fish, and some scientists prefer to call them, more properly, gelatinous zooplankton. They're durable, surviving wide ranges of environmental conditions. Around the world, as fish populations decline and pollution strikes, numbers of jellyfish have been observed to increase, often dramatically. (Once, in a British Columbia bay used for corralling huge rafts of logs, I motored around jellyfish as thick as blooming daisies in an underwater garden—beautiful but a sure signal that water quality was compromised.) An increasingly acidic ocean could favor jellyfish over other, more sensitive species, until perhaps the ocean becomes a jellyfish sea. Marine geochemist Richard Feely refers to this possibility as "evolution in reverse," the ocean returning to an earlier state with a much less diverse occupancy.

As the jellyfish sinks away from us, we turn back to our work. It's a slow, too slow, gathering of pattern to help explain this gorgeous, life-giving water world and what, without this faithful tedium and the public's understanding and acceptance of the data's meaning, it may become.

DAVID STUART MACLEAN
The Twittering Machine

In Donald Barthelme's "The School," you end up in a classroom where everything dies. The orange trees, the snakes, the tropical fish, the salamanders, the puppy, the Korean orphan, the grandparents, the parents, even some of the students. In just two pages, the story has the momentum of a howitzer, piling the bodies up in an inverted pyramid of importance. The teacher tells the story and he does it with the boozy intimacy of last call. The children in the story get disillusioned by the incongruity of their position: all this death and they were stuck in school. The children ask the teacher to make love to his assistant, so they can have, in their words, "an assertion of value." The teacher protests, then acquiesces, he and the assistant kiss, there's a knock at the door, a gerbil walks in, the children go wild with happiness.

I taught this story to a class of rising sixth-graders last summer. As a teacher, I have a bad habit of only wanting to talk about what I am currently excited about, a strategy guaranteed to teach my students nothing but how to have a conversation with a vaguely unhinged personality manically obsessed with a topic. It's problematic, but I have no alternative other than actually preparing a lesson plan, and that isn't going to happen any time soon.

If you want to examine emotional scarring, talk with a class of sixth-graders about death and suffering. They're geniuses on the subject. Each of my students had a story, of a relative, pet, or classmate, who died suddenly. They all knew they had been lied to about the deaths. Pria wanted to know how, on the drive home from the vet's after the family dog was put down, her mother was able to laugh and cry at the same time. Everyone was confused and scared, and it was beautiful. We all looked suffering and death in the face and none of us had any answers. I told them that it was hard and it got harder and then it gets easier, but I lacked the language to tell them why. Then, instead of a gerbil walking into the classroom, we went to recess.

It had pretty much the same effect. We escaped the classroom, which felt pressurized by our conversation, and immersed ourselves in the syrupy heat of a Houston summer and the constant conversation of our peers. The twittering machine of wild happiness that is fifteen minutes on the playground.

I got in trouble, of course. Not because of the disturbing conversation about the nature of death. But because of the three lines in the story about "making love." I was counseled to teach age-appropriate material.

I run nearly every day. My other hobby is aging, which I am also committed to doing every day. Each day, I try to be a little bit older than the day before. My two hobbies intersect in weird ways: I try to run faster on a body that's older, and currently the lower half of my body wants me to choose between my hobbies. I end up thinking about death a lot when I run. I think about my heart, distended from bourbon and marbled with tobacco tar, exploding. I think about my knees disassembling, and as I crash onto the gravel path, I imagine my body shattering like a champagne flute. I think about my lungs escaping through my mouth and hiding in the trees like helium balloons.

I try to keep my running habit a secret. Having spent my teen years in the early nihilist nineties, I am hardwired to distrust anyone who has a work ethic. I run at night on a path mostly populated by muggers and this one gorgeous transsexual who walks her giant gray camel of a dog slowly around the park. She has magnificent fur-covered boots that shiver with each of her steps. I run slowly and I run ugly. I have sweat glands embedded in sweat glands and I become slick as a dolphin within minutes of a jog. I spit a lot of mucus-y things that have the color and consistency of fetal birds. Sometimes in a fit of misguided self-esteem, I take my shirt off. The blood drains from my chest as I run, which allows the chest hair I do have to take on the allure of mange.

In a fit of enthusiasm, I signed up for a 10K race in Austin I'd read about online. I figured I could do a smaller race and perhaps retain some dignity as long as I did it in another zip code.

I drove into Austin the night before the race and stayed with my friend Rebecca. I knew her from a year we had spent together in India six years earlier. Rebecca has hair like a pile of cursive writing. We'd been at a conference years ago with a bunch of people, all of us sharing rooms with strangers, and Rebecca pulled me aside one night and asked, "Is your roommate the kind of guy who if I asked him if he'd take me into the bushes and fuck me he'd do it?"

She had a little apartment in the Hyde Park area of Austin, near the university. We chatted. Made plans for the evening. She made some jerk chicken and broccoli and rice. The chicken was good but the rice and broccoli were underdone. I used our conversation as a way to cloak my non-plate-cleaning behavior, given the broccoli situation. She told me about her father, who had been in a car accident two weeks prior. No big deal. He'd been broadsided, a crack in his spine, some internal bleeding, but he was due out of the hospital soon. He was supposed to have been released four days ago, but there was blood in his urine and he was going to be under observation a bit longer.

I told Rebecca about my mom and how she had broken her neck the previous year and was now perfectly fine. I think I made some provincial statement about the "amazing things they were doing in medicine nowadays," the kind of timeless cliché that's been breathlessly uttered throughout history about MRIs, shock therapy, and leeches.

We talked about relationships. She was in a new one, a good one. She showed me the cute thing he had written on her refrigerator's memo pad. It was a much better relationship than her last one, which was with a mean-spirited poet. Her father had written her a formal letter of protest over that boyfriend. I told her about my most recent dating debacle and how I was planning on becoming a monk. We joked about how relationships were all well and good, but the sex and extra attention did intrude on our sleep.

We looked at pictures from India and we talked about how young and skinny we looked. We mooned over pictures of each other and laughed about the aggressive mango sellers in front of the Charminar. Rebecca lit a cigarette and I decided that I was going to go ahead and smoke as well. Screw the race, I was here with my pal, Rebecca.

The phone rang.

Her mother was calling from the hospital. The doctors had pushed her into the grief room and told her to call a friend. Rebecca's father had coded.

"What does that mean, 'coded'?"

Rebecca sat on the couch and rocked. I knelt beside her and put my hand on her foot.

"Who's there with you, Mom?"

I got up and sat on the couch and put my arm around her. I rubbed her neck.

"What do you mean you don't have any friends?"

She and her mother went back and forth for a while, but it was too early in the crisis for there to be any definite clarity. Her father was being helped up to go to physical therapy. He fell to his knees in the hallway and began to code out on the floor. We still didn't know the definition of the verb in that sentence, and Rebecca hung up without getting it clear.

Rebecca pushed her face into my chest and cried. I wished I had giant breasts that she could smoosh her face into. My chest was too anemic to provide real comfort. I told Rebecca that there were lots of skilled people working very hard to help her father, that we had to trust them and their abilities right now. I took her cigarette from her and pushed it into the narrow capers jar she used for an ashtray.

"It's a hospital in Long Island. How skilled could they be," she asked. She glanced at the dinner table. "You didn't eat your dinner."

"We were *talking*."

"It was terrible, wasn't it?"

"The broccoli was a little raw."

"I'd feel better if I knew you weren't starving."

"I had some Arby's on the way here. I'm fine."

"That makes me feel better."

"I'm fine, really."

"I'll microwave it, not that you have to eat it, just so that it'll be ready." She put the plate in the microwave and zapped it for thirty seconds.

Her brother called. Her father was dead.

Rebecca threw herself onto the bed and got under the covers. She sat up, then she went down again. She put a pillow over her head. Her brother was on the way to the hospital. He had just parked and was walking toward the hospital. A beggar was waylaying him, he said into his cell phone.

"Mark, walk away. Just walk away from him. Mark, I need to ask you…Did you get away from him? Stop talking to him. Mark. Walk away from him."

I cleared the table.

There was a beeping in the room, every few seconds another beep. I couldn't find where it was coming from, so I climbed into bed with Rebecca and held her as she continued to yell at her brother, who wouldn't stop talking to the beggar. I wanted to give Rebecca her space. I wanted to hold her. I wanted to grab the phone out of her hand and sort through all of this business with her brother, real man-to-man brass tacks, get the lay of the land. I wanted to slip out the door and stand on her narrow balcony. Rebecca stood up and went into the bathroom and ran the faucet. The beeping continued.

I pulled out my laptop and started looking up flights to New York. I went to tell Rebecca that the earliest I could get her out was at seven the next morning. Nonstop, three hundred dollars. Rebecca was sitting on the edge of the full bathtub. The water was up to her knees. Her back was convulsing. It was the pose of someone fishing.

"You want to fly into Long Island, right?"

"That's like an hour away."

"JFK?"

Her apartment's in a complex, and the bathroom had the fluorescent white-walled anti-charm that breeds in those places. Rebecca was wearing white jeans, a white kurta, and black socks. Aside from the shampoo bottles, her black socks were the only color in the room. It felt like a Kubrick version of outer space. I brought her a cigarette.

I sat outside the bathroom and composed a to-do list with Rebecca, who remained with her feet in the bath. She had to pay her rent. She had to contact her graduate coordinator. She had a lot of produce that I should take. Dishes to wash. Pack. A key to mail her boyfriend so he could water her plants.

"Mark said to bring dressy clothes. What does he mean by that?"

Rebecca pulled off her socks and left them in the bottom of the full tub. She toweled off her legs and started piling clothes in a carry-on while I talked to another Rebecca, this one in Utah from JetBlue. I was confirming the reservation and also angling for a discount, some kind of bereavement fare. I told her the story. She told me it was a shame and the same price. Seven a.m. was when her flight left. It was 11:30 p.m. We'd have to leave by 5:15 to get to the airport on time. Both of us were guessing. I had never been to the Austin airport. Rebecca didn't have a car.

I started to wash the dishes. My cell phone rang. It was Ranjana, a friend of mine from Houston. She wanted me to call my friend Dan because Dan's friend Jeff had just been found dead in his apartment. I wasn't friends with Jeff. I knew him enough to buy him a beer once in a while. But I knew Dan, and I knew how his depression was always close by, ready to curdle up his system.

The word was Jeff was getting an autopsy. Ranjana said it just like that: Jeff is getting an autopsy, with Jeff in the subject position. Like Jeff is getting a root canal, Jeff is getting a tan blazer. Jeff is getting an autopsy because Jeff doesn't know how he died. That beeping was still going on.

I explained to Ranjana that I was a little bit busy at the moment, but then I just fell apart and started crying. I thought about the Barthelme story. Things were just piling up dead. I washed the dishes.

"You should wear the gloves."

Rebecca came into the small kitchen, found the cigarettes, and lit one.

"I don't mind dishpan hands," I said.

The thing about the Barthelme story is that, at the end, after all that death, the gerbil walks in. I was washing the dishes, desperate for the gerbil to walk in.

"It was stupid of my father to have kids at forty-seven. He should have known this was going to happen."

"How did your mom and dad meet?"

"On a beach in Acapulco. She had broken up with her boyfriend. She was a flight attendant. My dad saw her on the beach and bought her a pineapple."

There was another beep. I tried to act as if I hadn't heard it, just in case her apartment was falling apart.

"Are you ever going to turn this microwave off?" Rebecca snapped.

I knew my friend Dan would be taking Jeff's death hard. All obsessive early-risers, we were part of a group that met for coffee and did the crossword in the morning. Jeff worked security freelance and, on days he was working, he would show up in a black shirt tucked into black Carhartts tucked into black military boots with a flashlight, a knife, and a gun strapped to various places on his body. It had always been a little terrifying to see someone fully armed before I'd had my coffee. He'd joke about his personal armory. He could describe a gun's inner workings and what exact wound each kind of bullet would result in with such delicate detail that I'd forget we were talking about steel and bodies.

Rebecca and I spent the rest of the night smoking and talking about how we should quit smoking. I crashed out around two. I doubt Rebecca got any sleep. I barely remember the drive to the airport. It was dark and empty, and the traffic lights all blinked yellow.

At the airport, what could be said? I told her I loved her and wished her safe travels. She told me she loved me and wished me good luck in my race.

I had her keys and crashed at her place before the race started. Before I left, I drained the bathtub and hung her black socks on the shower rod. Her apartment was so small the sucking sound of the drain could be heard in every room.

At the race, fifteen thousand of us lined up waiting for the gun, all of us wearing the red technical shirts that were our race numbers. A sea of us all looking alike. I had barely slept, I had chain-smoked all night, I was exhausted. Everybody looked so beautiful in their expensive shoes and complicated wicking shorts. Their calves and arms looked expensive. It was going to be another race where I was the ugliest, where I was going to be the one who pulled off to walk, and to cough and spit and vomit on the side by the pylons.

I wanted a gerbil to walk in. I wanted to cheer.

I did terribly in the race. My lungs were paper bags.

*

When I was ten years old, a girl in the chorus of the summer play I was in was riding her bike on Olentangy River Road. Hilly terrain and teenagers in their parents' cars liked to go fast for the momentary lift behind the crest of every hill. Danielle got hit. Died.

She was Jewish and so had to be buried immediately. My mother didn't have enough time to make a thoughtful decision and so took me to the funeral. We stood there at the side of the grave. I had no idea what being Jewish entailed. I was ten, and often when I was asked my heritage, instead of saying Norwegian or Scottish, I identified myself as "Lettuce" because it had a similar sound.

At the grave, everyone around me started chanting in another language. I was the youngest child and was used to everyone speaking in ways that I didn't understand, but this was different. I hadn't ever heard these sounds before. Death seemed to entail a language that I knew nothing about. Danielle's mother was screaming these new words. She collapsed to the ground in her black dress. I remember thinking that even screaming and crying, she was beautiful. Everyone scooped dirt into the grave, including me. I was part of burying my friend. Complicit and didn't even know the language.

They had a wake for Jeff at an Irish bar down the street from my tiny apartment in Houston. The patio had been reserved for us. Jeff's girlfriend had been the one to find him, and the autopsy still hadn't come back, so none of us knew how he died. And he had no medical insurance, so there was a doubt that we'd ever know how he died, because who was going to pay for an autopsy? Jeff was estranged from everyone he was related to.

He was broke when he died. It seemed the wake was populated by his creditors. Some were owed thousands of dollars. The bar had an unpaid tab of his that was in triple digits. Nobody was dressed up. We all wore black T-shirts, smoked cigarettes, and drank. Dan showed up and I bought him a drink.

A man who was as wide as he was tall came out onto the porch. I heard him tell a story about someone calling him, wanting to know if he knew anyone in Tajikistan. "I told the guy I knew one person, but he was a Nazi, and not some skinhead, but a genuine old man Nazi."

Jeff's girlfriend stood up and asked for us to tell stories about Jeff. People told about Jeff losing his teeth all over town. He had had a partial set that fit badly and seemed to fall out every time he puked. People told the jokes Jeff told about rape, about pederasty. The man who knew the Nazi in Tajikistan got up and said, "I can't tell you all the details about this, since the statute of limitations hasn't expired yet."

It seems that his teenage daughter had gotten into some trouble because of an ex-boyfriend, and they needed to straighten him out. He called Jeff and they drove over to the high school. As they were walking up to the building, he asked Jeff, "You strapped?" and Jeff said, "Hell yes." They walked right through the metal detectors and didn't blink when they beeped. Jeff said to the approaching security guard, "We need to speak with Ronald Lewis." The security guard went and got the boy for them. They slammed this high-school kid against the lockers and threatened him with a nine-millimeter, told him if he ever messed around with his daughter again, they would kill him.

We all laughed. It's a perfectly reprehensible story. But that night we all laughed. I was desperate for it. In the sticky Houston heat, we drank and smoked the entire night. The next morning, after all the damage I had done to my body the previous night, I put on my shoes and my tiny shorts, and tried again to run faster.

THOMAS MALLON
Forty More Years: Nixon and Me

From my diary, April 22, 1994:

> ...came home to the news that Richard Nixon, a man who let me down again and again, and to whom I felt deeply connected—whether I was wearing a Nixon-Lodge button at the age of 9, or having a shouting match with my father over the Cambodian invasion ten years after that—had died; at 9:08 p.m., at the age of 81. There was never a time in my life when he wasn't on the scene; he was already a Senator when I was born. And now he's gone, and I sat before the television sobbing.

For all their supposed intimacy, diaries frequently fail to tell a whole or even essential truth, and this entry from mine, considered at a remove of eighteen years, surely conveys neither. What did I mean by "deeply connected"? Why exactly did I sob? Simply from a sense of Nixon's public longevity ("never a time in my life when he wasn't on the scene")? Ridiculous. Having recently turned sixty, I'm still experiencing that kind of celebrity departure: Elizabeth Taylor was already famous, even divorced, before I was born. I had only positive feelings for her—not so with Nixon—but I didn't sob at the news she was gone. We were long, friendly acquaintances who'd never met. Nixon—whom I did meet, once, for seconds—was an exhausting life partner.

My next few diary entries get no closer to the truth of things between us. I see strains of punditry and politics driving my pen on the day after Nixon's death:

> decided that [he] was probably the most interesting American of the last fifty years, and will loom large in histories a half century from now, when Kennedy will have become a minor romantic legend.

"Interesting": that least interesting of words, a tarpaulin to throw over anything you'd prefer to deal with later, or not at all. I'm not saying anything untruthful in these pompous lines, but I'm not revealing anything, either—unless one detects a belligerent note in that dismissal of JFK. The conservative side of my politics is coming through, and I appear to be warming up to a Nixonian defense of Nixon against his most famous, privileged, and overrated foe. Even so, I don't seem willing to carry RN's chip very far on my own shoulder.

The next day, April 24, I'm cranky over the newspaper and television obituaries, even with their approval of the China trip and détente:

What they will never praise him for is his early anti-Communism. That's something he always has to be shown 'outgrowing.' Well, he never outgrew it, not with the realpolitik *opening to China, not with the treaties with the Soviets. He was right about Hiss and the rest of them—all that ugly bunch...*

Well, I make no apologies for this. My anticommunism remains firm, fervent, and nostalgic. (Oh, for the old bipolar world!) But this entry, rather than coming to terms with Nixon, gets lost in his enemies, as Nixon so often did himself.

The funeral took place on Wednesday, the 27th, and I watched it on C-Span, my diary taking refuge in armchair reportage, comedy and, at last, sentimentality:

So many bizarre sights: Liddy! Agnew! Danny [Quayle]! No one can get over how wonderful Julie and [her brother-in-law] Eddie Cox look, or how unkind the years have been to Tricia and David [Eisenhower]...Poor Reagan looked very out of it—staring at nothing, with an open mouth, probably thinking he was on the set for Cattle Queen of Montana. *(And yet, when everyone stood for "The Star-Spangled Banner," he mouthed all the words.) The thing that touched me most: they put on the porch light of that little frame house. Richard Nixon was home. R.I.P.*

My diary was trying to give him, and our relationship, a decent, hasty burial.

Only in the past few years, while writing a long novel about the Watergate scandal, have I exhumed the tormented nexus of Nixon and me, performed a long-deferred autopsy on it, like the court-ordered exhumations demanded by conspiracy theorists. And I've *found* a conspiracy of sorts: a decades-long collusion between me and the corpse, rooted in my early absorption not only of Nixon's politics but of his personality too.

I mention, in that first entry, the Nixon-Lodge button. I can't find it now, but I remember wearing it to school, fourth grade, during the fall of 1960. That year's election night is my first important political memory. The returns began badly for my man, and I went from the living room into the kitchen—afraid to embarrass myself in front of my mother and sister?—for a chat with my father, a onetime New Dealer who had already taken Ronald Reagan's right turn toward political Damascus. I confessed to him my anxiety and disbelief: could Nixon, so much more *experienced* than his opponent, really be in danger of losing? My dad, a low-key humorous Irishman without a shred of ethnic or religious pride in the candidacy of John F. Kennedy, told me, gently, that it looked that way.

During the 1960s, a Nixon *supporter* joked about the perennial candidate as having been "forty-two years old the day he was born... other kids got footballs for Christmas, Nixon got a briefcase and he loved it." And your point? I thought, when I first heard this line. My childhood—unshadowed by tuberculosis and early death; governed by a merry father instead of a martinet—was much happier than Nixon's. But I, too, was a studious striver: first in my class and last to be picked for anything after school; popular enough to have a handful of cool friends, but ashamed of my efforts to acquire them. Bent upon success, I was also half in love with failure—and reaction. I played George III and Jefferson Davis in school debates, and in scanning the contemporary scene came to admire Nixon the fighter, the patient comeback artist. I was unaware that his own thrill in getting up from the mat probably depended on the equal or greater thrill he derived from the blow that preceded it.

Nixon appeared on Jack Paar's Friday night television program on March 8, 1963, four months after his second big defeat, in the California governor's race. I was watching. After chatting with the host, the former vice president played the piano, a brief sugary classical piece he'd written himself. When he finished, one could see Paar, off to the side and out of Nixon's sight, urging the audience toward greater applause, out of what I recognized even then as pity. Had it come to that?

I kept track of him over the next few years, during and after a more straightforward infatuation with Barry Goldwater, as Nixon made his way back, campaigning for all those congressional candidates who a few years later would owe him their support. I saw him appear on *Laugh-In* ("Sock it to *me?*"), trying to impress the cool kids, and I shook his hand—Pat's too—when they came through town during the '68 campaign. On November 5, I went to bed with my transistor radio at my ear, determined to stay awake until he definitively edged past Hubert Humphrey. The Lodge button from eight years before that may be gone, but I still have a one-sided vinyl record of Richard Nixon's convention acceptance speech from '68, in which he talks of himself as a boy who "hears the train go by at night and…dreams of far away places where he'd like to go."

I went off to college ten months later, all in favor of him and his policy of "winding down the war" via "Vietnamization." In my high-school valedictorian's speech, I had praised this middle course between "unacceptable extremes of surrender and slaughter," and I now defended Nixon in dormitory bull sessions, ignored the antiwar "Moratorium" days and voted against the call for a student strike during the convulsive month of May 1970.

But he was making things impossible for me. We were getting out of Vietnam but going *into* Cambodia? Did he have to drop his g's, as if he were one of his own "hardhat" supporters, when referring, three days before Kent State, to the "bums" who were "blowin' up the campuses"? Being for him began to feel not counterintuitive, but freakish; I pulled back, quarreled with my father about what "his" man was now doing. I think I actually scrawled "Return to Sender" across one letter from home, scorning my old man the way Nixon was scorned by the student demonstrators he visited in the middle of the night at the Lincoln Memorial. I was eighteen years old, frightened, and worn out by the Age of Aquarius. Nixon was frightened too. Little more than a ring of empty buses protected the White House from the hundreds of thousands of protestors in Washington, and he took to running the government from his fortified mountaintop lodge at Camp David.

In the end, he was largely the one who calmed things down. The troops continued to come home, albeit slowly, and the President pursued a domestic agenda that was in many respects—a guaranteed national income, universal medical insurance, heavy increases in arts funding—more liberal than anything Bill Clinton or Barack Obama would eventually put forward. "Watch what we do, not what we say," his attorney general, John Mitchell, remarked in a burst of political candor not since equaled.

And, of course, Nixon went to China. Here I am on February 28, 1972, trying to sound clever about it in the diary: "At this moment the only thing I would say is clear is that Taiwan Savings Bonds are not an especially good buy." But this entry also contains my own wary peace feeler to the man I'd stepped away from two years before. It's offered as part of a compliment to Mrs. Nixon's progress through Peking: "She was lovely and warm throughout. In one way, the Nixons are better at this sort of ice-breaking than anyone else. They always feel they are a little out of their league, it seems, always cautious and a little unsure of themselves, because of their backgrounds, defeats, etc. It helps them avoid any arrogance abroad. At home?" I can't say much for my grammar here, or for that little rhetorical question—hedging my bets—at the end of the passage. But I do hear something more revealing in these few sentences than in any of what I would write two decades later, after his death. I hear the voice of the scholarship student, the self-doubter, the boy who, if *he* were going to China, would read every briefing book twice, as I'm sure Nixon did himself, rather than trying to get by on his small natural allotments of charm and charisma.

The president ended the draft in June 1973, just as my class was graduating. We were secretly grateful but derived entertainment during our last weeks on campus from watching the sudden barrage of Watergate developments on the evening news. After a decade of urban riots, assassination and napalm, the hapless burglary and cover-up felt like guffaw-worthy comic relief. (I remember my father, ready to go down with Nixon's ship, breaking ranks for only a moment to ask me: "Liddy is a weirdo, isn't he?") The scandal played itself out for another year, until the resignation in August 1974, the only month of my life when I've ever been seriously sick. Some ferocious sort of food poisoning persisted in me for weeks, rendering me gaunt and dangerously dehydrated. By the time I woke up in the hospital, the fever at last broken, Jerry Ford was in the White House toasting his own English muffins. Our "long national nightmare" was over, and I subsided back toward health, left with the literary luxury to wonder whether my body somehow hadn't been playing empathetic host to Nixon's death throes.

I don't, in fact, believe in the psychosomatic to such an extent, but—to go back to that 1994 diary—there *was* something that "deeply connected" me to Richard Nixon; not to the darkest parts of his nature but to the man who craved burial for its opportunities of resurrection. The subtext of that closing line on April 22—my sobs over Nixon's death—is really a super-text, the words that *begin* the entry's rigorously chronological account of that day. In the morning, I'd suffered an ordinary little career setback, the collapse of a magazine assignment that had been presented to me as a sure thing and on which I had worked very hard. "Well, the hell with them," I wrote, after describing "their" editorial perfidy at some length. "I have been badly used..."

That's our boy! They wouldn't have Mallon to kick around any more. I was already figuring out the comeback for this piece ("One thing I won't do is butcher it down to a thousand words"); was already, before the day was over, back "in the arena," as Nixon liked to say, quoting Theodore Roosevelt. I was trying "not to let this get me too down," as my partner and I went out that evening to hear some music at the Café Carlyle, about twenty blocks from where Nixon was dying. But it's not in me to take my mind off disappointment, and I remained raw, more so than I thought, throughout our hours at the nightclub. It was this wounded, I'll-show-'em mood that triggered those sudden sobs when we arrived home to the news from New York Hospital. Richard Nixon: *mon semblable, mon frère!* Alas, *he* would never again have the chance to show them.

How many books of mine he turns up in! The White House tapes appear in my study of diaries, discussed as the ultimate example of a secret journal whose discovery sets in motion someone's undoing. In a scene from *Fellow Travelers,* a novel, Nixon is there at Joe McCarthy's wedding, speaking more or less the words he actually said to reporters, coming out of the church on September 29, 1953: "The bride was lovely, but then I've never met a bride who wasn't!" I could hardly improve upon this maladroit combination of attempted suavity and unconscious offense, and so, after quoting it, I have one reporter murmur to another: "Did he just insult Joe's wife?" And there he is in *Yours Ever,* a much-later companion to the diaries book, where I briefly ponder Nixon's wartime letters from the South Pacific to Pat: "You'll never know how proud I was to show [your picture] to all the fellows," he wrote her. "Everybody raved—wondered how I happened to rate! (I do too.)" Did he ever.

An editor once took me to lunch to ask if I'd consider writing a short biography of Lincoln for a series he oversaw. I rejected the idea pretty quickly; I'd just published a novel about the other couple in the box at Ford's Theatre on the night of the president's assassination, but really, what could I bring to a Lincoln biography that hadn't already been brought by a hundred biographers before me? So we moved on to other topics of conversation, but as we left the restaurant, I found myself saying: "Please don't ever give away Nixon without at least calling me."

I suppose I was sneaking up to the subject, circling it, for thirty years. By 2003 I was living in Washington, across the street from the Watergate, that complex of curved buildings Nixon claimed never to have passed, let alone entered. Few things are more elusive than the origins of a novel, but after several years of looking through my study window at the scene of the crime, I started work on the longest book of fiction I've ever written, a narrative that covers the whole claustrophobic little epic that was Watergate, from the break-in to the pardon. My editor urged me to move away from my usual practice of fictionalizing big events through the viewpoints of minor characters or bystanders—that couple in Lincoln's box, for instance—and, for this one, to get inside the heads of the central players, including the most central of all. *Watch what we do, not what we say.*

So I've spent most of the past three years with Nixon, wallowing in Watergate, sometimes letting his voice be the last one I hear before going to sleep. Many of the White House tapes are up on YouTube, endlessly looping, being heard by somebody, somewhere, at every moment in time, as if they were "Moon River" or "After You've Gone." They leave a listener enthralled and revolted, not just by the nastiness of Nixon's bigotry or what Nixon himself called the "gangster language" of his confederates, but also by the crude dullness of his musings on almost any subject but foreign policy.

His talents in that realm had much to do with the tapes' creation and preservation: so long as they remained playable, no one, he surely thought, would be able to argue that anyone but Nixon himself had conceived his administration's grand designs. Indeed, to watch Nixon conducting foreign affairs on a visionary level during the worst and most preoccupying months of Watergate is to marvel at his capacities for concentration and, perhaps, dissociation. Listening to the tapes that pertain to Watergate itself, one realizes that far from trying to cover up what knowledge of the scandal he actually has, Nixon is trying to demonstrate *more* knowledge than he possesses; trying to convince his aides that he remembers who worked where and did what; trying to make the staffers with whom he's now conspiring believe that he's more on top of things than he is.

I've tried to comprehend those weeks in the spring of 1970—the empty buses like a moat around the White House—from his vantage point and his wife's, in order to understand the lust for control that the experience engendered: the Plumbers, the break-ins, the Enemies List. But I find myself more absorbed by the muted nature of his reaction to triumph, especially his massive win in November of '72, twelve years after a hair's-breadth loss and four years after a hair's-breadth win.

Finally he had a majority to exceed even those won by Eisenhower, his patron. And yet, the immediate experience left him subdued, even downcast. On election night he was also experiencing discomfort from the loss of a cap that had been fitted to one of his front teeth in 1947. A dentist had to be summoned to the White House to make temporary repairs before the president could go across town and greet his cheering supporters ("Four more years! Four more years!") at the Shoreham Hotel. In my novel I imagine Nixon in the basement dispensary, being attended to by Dr. Chase:

> He felt an odd desire to go upstairs and find the old cap, which had disappeared into the carpet. It seemed like some telltale clue he had left behind, and he felt, despite the replacement, somehow incomplete without it...he couldn't take his mind off the letdown he was feeling. Rose [Mary Woods] was having to fight it, too; he could tell that when he saw her getting off the plane at Andrews. Only Pat seemed genuinely happy. He tried for a moment to think of the election as a gift to her—it meant, after all, no more politics. But he didn't suppose there was much logic in giving thanks to politics for putting an end to itself; sort of like thanking God for sparing some people in the earthquake He'd just caused. Why not just dispense with the quake to begin with?
>
> But it was not 1947, and he could not stop the life that he himself had set in motion. He went upstairs to look for the artificial tooth through which he'd spoken his first words in Congress.

What he was realizing—in the recesses of a subconscious he probably didn't believe in—was that the only way he could ever again run for office, and thereby feel fully himself, was to *lose* the election he'd just won by a landslide. He felt, I'm certain, not the joy of victory or any imminence of the disaster that would soon engulf him, but the first approach of death.

KIMBERLY MEYER
What the Desert Said

At the beginning of the third book of the *Odyssey,* Telemachus' ship pulls into the harbor of sandy Pylos, as the morning light burnishes the sea. Homer tells us:

> *The sun rose from the still, beautiful water*
> *Into the bronze sky, to shine upon the gods*
> *And upon men who die on the life-giving earth.*

Although that sun dawns upon gods and men alike, this is how we humans are defined: as those who die. We are not the gods, the *athanatoi,* as the Greek has it—the ones beyond death, and therefore beyond time. Instead, we are bound by time. We may once have walked in a garden with the Lord of all creation, but we've been banished to a land of thorn and thistle, and the life-giving earth from which we were made now folds us back into its dust at the end of our days. The time of timelessness is over.

And yet the ache for that state of timelessness remains. We seek it in sacred places, which mark off a space from the ravages of the time-bound world that our mortal bodies inhabit. When Yahweh calls out to Moses from the midst of the bush that burned with fire but was not consumed, he is marking off sacred space—the place where He will appoint Moses to lead the Israelites out of Egypt and to their homeland of Canaan. "Draw not nigh hither," Yahweh commands, "put off thy shoes from off thy feet, for the place whereon thou standest is holy ground." So holy that *seneh,* the Hebrew word for "bush," perhaps even gave the Sinai its name. When, centuries later, the Roman Empress Helena ordered that a Chapel of the Burning Bush be built at the base of Mount Sinai to commemorate this moment, she too was marking off sacred space. And when the miracle is remembered by pilgrims who travel to the desert to put off their shoes and stand inside that church, it is still happening, it is always happening, and time, and our subjection to it, is, therefore, annulled.

Last summer, my daughter, Ellie, and I attempted to retrace the path of one such pilgrim, a Dominican priest from Ulm, Germany, who traveled to the Holy Land and Mount Sinai in 1483. This friar, Felix Fabri, wrote an account of his journey, one filled with tangible details—traversing the dry Judean hills by donkey, paying tolls to the Saracen lords of Jerusalem, kissing the bodily relics of saints—of travel in the Age of Faith. I'd stumbled across his *Book of Wanderings* in the library years before and been inexplicably transfixed. My preoccupation seemed in some ways especially mystifying given the precarious state of my immortal soul, which had been in self-imposed exile from the Kingdom of God for the better part of my life. All that time, I stood on the outside of faith, my face peering in through the bars of the gates of the garden, while the cherubim with their whirling swords of flame kept me at bay. But in my exile, I was haunted. By God, maybe. Or maybe by a longing for evidence to refute my fear that this material world is all there is. Perhaps God and this longing are one. It's not that I thought I would find either God or solace for my fears by retracing Fabri's path. I knew that he traveled through a world still enchanted by belief, a world that for me was irrevocably shorn of magic and miracles. And yet I went.

A restlessness seemed to drive Fabri. "I call God to witness that for many years I was in such a fever of longing to perform that pilgrimage that whether I was asleep or awake I hardly ever had any other subject before my mind," Fabri writes. "And I may say with truth that while engaged in these thoughts I lay awake for more than a thousand hours of the night and time of rest." A similar restlessness had driven me. For almost two months, my daughter and I followed Fabri from Ulm to Venice, where he had boarded a pilgrim galley. We followed him as he sailed along the Dalmatian Coast and through Greece and Cyprus. We followed him through the port of Jaffa into Jerusalem, and then across the Negev. Here, on this very spot, we were told at all the churches and monasteries and historical monuments we visited, here, right here, touch it, bless your rosary upon it, a miracle occurred. Maybe a martyrdom. Maybe a sermon. Maybe a last supper. Maybe a birth or death or resurrection. By the time we reached Taba, where we crossed from Israel into the wilderness of the Sinai Desert on our way to

St. Catherine's Monastery and the Chapel of the Burning Bush, our capacity for wonder was severely frayed.

For days, we navigated the *wadi*s, dry riverbeds running through the desert, in the jeep of Sheik Swelam, a sinewy Bedouin, who brought with him his sullen twelve-year-old son, and Mohammad, an interpreter, fresh from the Revolution in Tahrir Square. As we drove across the bottom of what was once an ancient ocean, we stared out the open windows at pale sandstone formations, some crouched on the desert floor like sphinxes, some like fallen temples. The red stone hills in the distance seemed chiseled and carved as with a frieze. But the sphinxes, the temples, the friezes are just similes: *like* or *as*. In reality, there were no monuments here trying to stay the passage of time. No monuments marking anything at all. And in this vast desert, we seemed to be the only breathing, moving things. Everywhere, the relentless sun was shining upon men who die on the life-giving earth.

As Felix Fabri and his pilgrim band, led by an Arab guide, leave Gaza and that last outpost of civilization recedes behind them, the pitilessness of the terrain, their own relentless thirst, the breadth of the endless waste take hold. "In these plains we saw neither men nor beasts, neither villages, houses, trees, grass, nor bushes, but only the sandy earth, parched by the sun's heat," he writes on the 11th of September, 1483. In the afternoon, they enter a land of swelling hills. In the valley between them, the travelers pitch their tents. The camel drivers head off with jars and water-skins to fetch fresh water from a cistern, while the pilgrims spread out in search of firewood. They find only dry bushes—*seneh*—which they pull up by the roots.

"This place was called in Arabic *Chawatha*, and here we found many proofs that once human dwellings had stood there," Fabri writes, "for we found above us twelve great ancient walled cisterns, round about which lay many broken bricks, broken pots, and ashes from smiths' forges...In the cisterns we saw the dead bodies of great and terrible serpents, and of animals unknown to us." On the morning of the 12th, they load the camels early, before daylight, and depart from Chawatha together in the dark.

*

Although the days of camel caravans, like the days of miracles, are over, I had insisted on riding camels in the desert. So Sheik Swelam hired camels for us that first afternoon. Often we paused to let them graze on clumps of spiny grasses, their heads on their necks moving periscopically, their gaze, like their chewing, ruminative. We passed through an abandoned Bedouin camp, detritus of detritus: nylon fencing, wood scraps, oil drums, empty and tattered rice bags. Later we saw acacia trees tied with bits of fading fabric, precarious stacks of flat stones. "Signs," said Mohammad, though of what he did not say. Of the presence of humans? The way through the desert? Were these portents from the divine? We tried to read the engravings on the desert walls—camels and goats scratched into the sandstone surface, strange rows of vertical lines. What did they mean? There were fragments of Arabic too, nearly worn away—*Bismillahir Rahmanir Rahim, In the name of Allah, the Most Beneficent, the most Merciful.*

We came across a wizened elderly sheik and his plump young wife in the shadow of a rock formation, the shade like the curve of the lunula of a fingernail. They sat on a rug beside their jeep. When we pulled up, the woman covered her head. Over a small fire, she made us sweet tea in a tin vegetable can rinsed clean, then poured the tea into two small, clear glasses. Later, when we finished our tea and the glasses were rinsed and refilled for Sheik Swelam and Mohammad, and finally for the sullen son, I realized that these were the only ones they had. While Sheik Swelam and the couple talked, Ellie and I looked out on the endless floor of the former sea, lined by bisque-colored buttes and mesas, sky and sky and sky. Mohammad said the couple were speaking together in an older Arabic brought by their ancestors when these desert nomads came, like Abraham, with their camels and goats and their wool tents and woven rugs from Arabia centuries ago. In some unfathomable way that ancient tongue they spoke seemed connected to the faded etchings on the walls of the canyons. In the desert, time slowed and stretched—or maybe it condensed, thickening like a reduction in which all excess was boiled away. Or perhaps that is only how it was in my mind, or now, in my memory of it.

*

In the morning, Sheik Swelam, a cigarette dangling from his lips, makes milky Nescafé over a fire of a few twigs, washing out the clear glasses with a swill of water, elegantly whirling and rubbing with his thumb at the same time. We sit on the rugs from the jeep in silence, eating flatbread and soft white cheese and jam. Then all day we drive the wadis, stopping at a Bedouin camp where we all drink tea and Sheik Swelam and Mohammad smoke cigarettes with men possessed of piercing eyes and stained teeth. Later, in the shade of an acacia tree or a sandstone cliff, lunch and a rest. Then we drive on. From time to time, Sheik Swelam veers off the wadi to a well he remembers, and he fills the water jugs, protected by cloth covers embroidered by the women— distant figures against the hills in black shawls and long black robes, young children on their hips, surrounded by shaggy goats. At the wells, Sheik Swelam has Ellie and me bend over while he pours the cold water down our necks, wetting our hair, keeping us cool in the intense desert heat, heat like a kiln, heat without relief. Later in the afternoon, when Sheik Swelam spots a band of shrubs in the parched riverbeds, we get out of the jeep and, like the pilgrims, we gather dried branches of the desert bushes to burn. Toward evening, in a gully or in an encampment or at an oasis, Mohammad and the sheik and his wordless son pull out the sleeping bags and the food and the pots and plates, and while Ellie and I try to find a hidden place to wash the desert sand out of the pores of our faces, they cook for us—chicken and vegetables, flatbread, a thick fava bean stew. As the fire dies out, we fall asleep beneath the stars. No voice calls out to us from the midst of the burning.

For Fabri and the medieval pilgrims who made their punishing journey that late summer and early fall of 1483, the desert wilderness of the Sinai was sacred, the Word of God made Flesh. Although their bodies were at the mercy of this brutal place on the map, they crossed a spiritual landscape that existed beyond time, beyond the physical world that made their bodies suffer. As he travels, Fabri thinks about the symbolic nature of the desert. It is, he says, a wasteland, abandoned by God, "as though [He] had used it to improve or adorn the rest of the universe. The country," he goes on, "seems also forsaken by the heavens, for it lacks the kindly influence of the stars, and seems to be viewed angrily by them, and, as it were, turned into iron, while the heaven above seems harsh, pitiless, and brazen." Because of this harshness, he says, the desert has always been a site of testing and temptation. But it is also where God bestowed the laws upon Moses. It's where manna rained down. It's a place of retreat from the world, and of devotion and contemplation. You can be found here. At the same time, you can easily get lost, for through the desert there is no fixed path.

I never knew where I was in the desert. Not only were we untethered from time, we were untethered from space as well. As we passed from wadi to wadi, I wrote down their names in my notebook: Wadi Razala, Wadi Lathi, Wadi Watir. But without a map to pin them to, the names meant nothing. Sometimes I would try to orient myself with the traveling sun. But the direction we were going did not indicate the place where we were, which is what I wanted.

Lunch one day beneath a gnarled acacia tree, the only shade to be found. Tomatoes and cucumbers, canned tuna with chopped onions, white cheese, tea, unleavened bread. The only sounds: flies, the wind. Ellie and I lie on mats beneath the delicate leaves of the acacia and read. Sheik Swelam and Mohammad smoke cigarettes. The son sleeps in the jeep. I ask the sheik where, exactly, we are. With a stick, he draws a map in the dirt of where we've been, one wadi branching off into another, like a bare tree in winter. Looking out across the expanse of sand and scrub, he tells me he could travel this land day or night. "Everything I have in here," he says, tapping his head.

That night we camp in a ravine, at the point where two wadis meet, one flowing to the Suez Gulf, the other to the Gulf of Aqaba, a tipping point, a hinge of the earth. During dinner, cooked over the small fire pit, fueled by splinters of seneh we'd collected in the afternoon, Sheik Swelam points off to the Milky Way far south of us and says that when it's centered over the southern sky, the fruit of the date palms is most sweet.

I said no voice called out to us from the midst of the burning fire, but sometime in the night, I woke up in the darkness, shivering in the dry desert air. Maybe it was only the chill that sharpened my mind, but I opened my eyes to the clarity of the stars, near and bright and many as the descendants Yahweh promises to Abraham in Genesis. It seemed that I was not so much looking *at* things as looking *through* them to something beyond. The turning earth had carried the Milky Way straight above us by this still hour, and, for a moment, I thought I was looking at a topographical map of another world, the white, ridged cloud of the Milky Way like a chain of mountains, and the countless stars like the towns and villages and cities of a country I didn't know. I thought about that other world, gazing out at us, the desert I inhabited being its firmament and constellations, any life there looking up in wonder at us lying in these heavens of sand. How much is hidden, I thought, by the deceptive light of day. How little, I hoped, do we actually see of what exists.

"Everything I have in here," Sheik Swelam had said, like one of the ancient bards who sang from memory of gods and heroes and men who die on the life-giving earth. How lightly the Bedouin travel, how little they carry, how few marks they make. Everywhere on this trip, Ellie and I had seen monuments built by human hands to commemorate and mark and remember. Even Fabri's account was a shrine of memory, experience encased in words. "I never passed one single day while I was on my travels," he wrote to his Dominican brethren, "without writing some notes, not even when I was at sea, in storms, or in the Holy Land; and in the desert I have frequently written as I sat on an ass or a camel; or at night, while the others were asleep, I would sit and put into writing what I had seen."

I wanted to write it all down too—sweet tea made in a tin can and the curve of shade at the base of the curve of a mesa, a Bedouin woman, glint of black against the dun-colored sand, a sky punctured by stars. This attempt to pluck ephemera from the flux of experience and to pin them in words is the marking out of sacred space. It encloses the past, removes it from time, and tries to keep it alive in its own private Eden. But of course this is impossible—to capture any moment and take it home as a souvenir.

One morning, Fabri and his pilgrim band enter the region of Wadi el-Arish. On their right rise mountains of exceeding whiteness; on their left, an expanse of black stone and sand, "scorched as though a fire had lately burned everything that would burn therein." Fabri asks his guide where this wilderness ends, and the guide replies that no living man has ever been to the end of it. Because for Fabri this desert wilderness is sacred territory, because it is both spiritual and actual, he imagines that abutting the boundary of these plains must be the earthly paradise where time stands still, "and therefore the flashings of the fiery sword, which the Lord has placed before the entrance to paradise, has scorched these plains and forbids all approach." But paradise is manifestly there.

In the Sinai peninsula that my daughter and I crossed, the only monument is the desert itself, and what's remembered is only in the mind. A few marks on the rock walls, a few stacks of stones, bright rags tied in trees. The Bedouin who inhabit this precarious land seem to recognize of necessity how flimsy are the things made, how soon they will pass away. And this recognition is, it seemed to me as we drove over the impenetrable surface of it, a kind of submission to this essential fact of human existence: our fragility. We are the men who die on the life-giving earth.

After every meal, Sheik Swelam would scrape the plastic plates clean and wash them with water from the jugs we carried in the jeep, then throw what couldn't be saved into the fire. The scrapings he would leave on a flat stone for the desert animals.

This is what the desert said: Carry only what you need. Burn what can't be saved. Leave the remnants as an offering.

EILEEN POLLACK
Didn't Anyone Tell You

Last summer, with a serial rapist roaming Ann Arbor, I asked my undergraduates to read an essay called "In the Combat Zone" by Leslie Marmon Silko, in which she argues that if women felt comfortable using firearms, they wouldn't present such passive victims for men intent on harming them. One of my female students, fair and lithe as a stalk of goldenrod, informed me that she had nothing to fear from anyone; she had been a track star in high school, and if any man tried anything she didn't like, she could always outrun him.

I shuddered when I heard this, having said the same words to my mother when I was that age. Back then, I was sure my parents' prohibition against my living or traveling alone stemmed from nothing more than their old-fashioned sense that a woman was a fragile creature whose virginity needed to be protected, coupled with a willful denial of how resourceful I was. Though only five-four, I was fleet of foot and strong, and I had been trained by my older brother to withstand a tackle.

But even my brother shared their fears. "There's no man I couldn't get away from," I bragged, at which he came up from behind and lifted me from the ground. Kicking, flailing helplessly, I choked out an admission that I was wrong, then went on living as if I weren't.

The choices seemed stark—stay at home until I was safely coupled with a husband, or get out there and see and do all I wanted to see and do, denying the reality that I was far more at risk for getting hurt than my—stronger, fleeter, less sexually vulnerable—brother. I didn't need lessons on how to shoot a gun. What I needed were lessons on how to navigate—wisely, bravely—that first, terrifying year I was out of college.

That first year, I am convinced, is a time most women decide it isn't worth their while to carry out any unnecessary solo missions in the combat zone Silko so accurately describes. For my parents to have provided such lessons would have been to concede their approval of my plan to spend the summer working in Philadelphia and the two years after that studying in England and exploring Europe. (My mother was so upset at my announcement that I had won a Marshall Scholarship to study abroad that she shook her head sadly and said, "I'll break the news to your father.")

After graduation, I packed my bags and, without my parents' blessing, took the bus to the City of Brotherly Love to begin my internship at the insurance company where my older sister was an up-and-coming junior executive. She had been the first to test our parents' wariness about a woman living on her own. As an undergraduate at Barnard, she had been mugged in the Manhattan subway, but our parents seemed to worry far more about me than they did about her. She was the responsible, clear-headed sibling, while even in junior high I had shown a penchant for taking risks. Having earned her MBA from Wharton, my sister worked her way up the ladder at one of the largest insurance companies in the world. Although she was transferred to Atlanta, she finagled me a summer internship at the home office in Philadelphia and then found me a place to stay at a boarding house run by an elderly woman who used to work at the company. The neighborhood was poor and rundown, but the landlady, Mrs. Plummer, was a feisty raconteur who told me stories about the misdeeds of her former bosses, who were *my* bosses now. Clearly, she was one of those women who should have run a department rather than take dictation from the less competent men who did.

The only disadvantage was that Mrs. Plummer owned a cat that frequently vomited on my bed. The lock on my bedroom door didn't latch. But Mrs. Plummer assured me that I would be safe because the door that led in from the street was secured by two heavy deadbolts. The only other lodger was a grossly overweight and unhappy Finnish guy named Ron, who had been forced to drop out of Wharton for reasons as yet unclear to me. He claimed he managed a Radio Shack in the suburbs, but whenever I got home, he would be sitting in the living room, watching TV and drinking beer. He never said anything provocative, but I could tell that he resented me for holding a better job than he did, as he resented my sister for having earned her MBA from the same business school that kicked him out. "You wouldn't have this job if not for your connections," he grumbled, as if my sister and I belonged to some privileged Old Girl network rather than having grown up in a desolate town in upstate New York, the daughters of a dentist who himself had grown up poor; as if my sister hadn't been one of the very first women to earn a degree from Wharton; as if I didn't wear the same three hideously out-of-date suits—my sister's castoffs— in rotation every day and rent a room in the same crappy boarding-house as he did.

Still, I was determined to enjoy the summer. Undaunted by the hundred-degree heat or the endless sanitation strike that had left mountains of garbage rotting along the sidewalks, I spent all my spare time exploring the city. Of course, this was exactly the sort of behavior my parents feared. Back in the seventies, there was still an unspoken assumption—which quite frequently *was* spoken—that the greatest danger facing any white female lay in poor black neighborhoods. The racism inherent in such paranoia struck me as ugly and untrue, so I planned my excursions based on other considerations.

One weekend, I decided to visit the art museum, and rather than take the bus to Center City and walk north, I started walking due east. On and on I went through the blazing, garbage-mounded streets, until I found myself passing buildings that were burnt out or deserted. The neighborhood seemed devoid of habitation, but then, on one slightly less devastated block, I saw that each stoop was populated by a few shirtless black guys lolling in the heat. No woman would have relished passing through such a gauntlet, especially in the T-shirt and shorts I had on, but I didn't want to hurt the young men's feelings, so I made my way between them, nodding and saying "hey." Too tired and hot to move, they nodded almost imperceptibly and murmured "hey" or "how you doing."

As the weeks wore on, though, I began to absorb the fear rising from the streets with the heat and the stench of garbage. That was the summer the Philadelphia police laid siege to a black back-to-nature commune called MOVE, which had taken over a building in the same blighted neighborhood through which I had passed on my walk to the museum. Most black people felt little sympathy for MOVE's diatribes against zoos, cooked food, medicine, and technology. But the mayor's attempt to starve into submission a group that included pregnant women and toddlers raised the community's ire. Early in August, the cops stormed the compound. One officer was shot in the head, possibly by his own men. Most of the adults were arrested, and the violent beating of one MOVE member was recorded by a reporter's camera.

After that, the city grew so tense I suspected it was only a matter of time before something bad happened, although, as usually is the case, I wouldn't have predicted that the danger lay not among strangers, but among people I knew. One evening, I came home from work to find Ron in his usual spot. He offered me a beer. When I declined, he muttered, "Snob." I climbed the stairs, fixed dinner in Mrs. Plummer's kitchen, then showered in the bathroom Ron and I shared. Even when I switched on the fan in my bedroom window, the room remained stifling hot. Dejected, I took off my clothes and crawled beneath the sheet to sleep.

Only to be startled awake in the middle of the night by a two-hundred-and-fifty-pound naked white guy—Ron—towering above my bed.

There must have been a light outside—I remember the sickly radioactive glow of all that flesh. My first thought was to jump up and run, but I was naked beneath the sheet. Mrs. Plummer's bedroom was on the third floor, and with the fan clattering in my window, she wouldn't hear me scream. Not that I *could* scream. I was silenced by the terror that freezes you in a nightmare. I remember thinking: *So this is why people get killed. If you're really scared, you're too paralyzed to escape or fight.*

Ron, meanwhile, did nothing but stare down at me with such a scornful expression I wanted to cry out: *Why do you hate me? You don't even know me!* Then it occurred to me that he *did* know me, at least well enough to hate me. He hated me because I was a woman. Because I was more successful than he was. Because my sister had graduated from Wharton and gotten me an internship at the insurance company where she worked. Because I had refused to watch the game and share his beer.

"Ron," I said, "you don't want to do this." But apparently he did. Cock in hand, he pissed up and down the bed. The urine spattered the thin sheet covering my bare skin. I was so shocked I couldn't move. "Ron!" I shouted. "No!" He shook his head, as if startled from a dream, then turned and lumbered off.

I barricaded the door. I must have ventured out to take a shower, but how would I have found the courage? I know I balled the sheets and left them in an acrid heap beside the bed. I must have put on one of my sister's suits and taken the subway to work, because I was sitting at my desk when the cleaning crew came in to clean. I remember thinking I could never tell my parents, because they would blame me for sleeping in a room with a door that wouldn't lock. Nor could I tell my landlady. What was I supposed to say, "You know your other boarder, Ron? Well, he came in naked last night and peed all over me." It all was too embarrassing. I would, I decided, blame the wet sheets on the cat.

At nine, my sister called from Atlanta. I had no intention of confessing what had happened—like my parents, she would blame me for sleeping in an unlocked room. But the catatonia in my voice betrayed me. "What is it?" she said. "What's wrong?" I was afraid she would insist that I tell our parents—she did, in fact, chide me about the unlocked door—but she understood my reasons for not wanting to remind our parents why a young woman shouldn't be living alone. Instead, she made me promise I would tell my landlady. I gave my word, then hung up and called Mrs. Plummer. Horrified, she said she would take care of the matter, then called me back to report that she had issued an ultimatum: either Ron sign himself into rehab, or she would turn him over to the police. Apparently, he had no memory of what he had done, but he allowed Mrs. Plummer to drive him to a facility.

By the time I got home, she had washed the linens and remade the bed, but the cat had vomited on my pillow, and I decided I couldn't spend another night in that house. I quit my job and flew to Los Alamos to spend the rest of the summer with my boyfriend, Kevin. He and I met the summer before, working at Oak Ridge National Laboratory in Tennessee. Back then, nuclear weapons and reactors didn't scare me, but in the intervening year, I had left physics to become a writer, and within days of arriving at Los Alamos, I realized I could never live with a man who worked at a facility where nuclear weapons were manufactured. Dejected, I asked Kevin to drive me to the bus station in Albuquerque, where I used the last of my savings to buy a ticket home.

As if the summer hadn't been upsetting enough, a few miles outside El Reno, Oklahoma, a series of loud popping noises rang out and a bullet hole appeared in the window above my head. As the sheriff told us later, life in Oklahoma got so boring that the good ol' boys sometimes sat on the hill outside the Burger King with a six-pack of beer, taking pot shots at the Greyhound. I wasn't targeted as a woman—there were bullet holes above the heads of the two male passengers behind me. But the men on the bus, most of them foreign tourists, romanticized the shooting as a big adventure ("Cowboys!" they shouted. "Indians!"). I, on the other hand, had to hurry to the fetid restroom to heave up the rancid taco I had wolfed down two stops before.

I made it to my parents' house without further mishap and spent the next few weeks recuperating. I wanted to tell my mother about all the terrible things that had happened to me, but our unspoken agreement was that she and my father wouldn't ask why I had quit my job, why I had traveled to Los Alamos, why I had returned by bus weeks earlier than I had said I would be arriving, and I, in turn, wouldn't volunteer the information. Why bring any of it up? All they would say is: Didn't we tell you this is what happens to young women who insist on living on their own?

In September, I traveled to Washington, D.C., and took a cab to the British Embassy to meet my fellow Marshall Scholars. Exhilarated to be traveling abroad for the first time, I crossed the Atlantic with the group, and we passed a glorious day touring the Houses of Parliament. The other Marshalls were studying at Oxford or Cambridge, but I had chosen one of the newer, less stuffy universities where the term started later, so I stayed in London to sightsee. Amazed to be treading the same streets that Shakespeare, Dickens, and Virginia Woolf had trod, I walked until my feet were blistered raw. At a first-aid station in the Tower of London, a nurse pronounced the wounds infected, and I needed to be transported to the offices of a foot surgeon to have my feet tended and wrapped in gauze.

Undaunted, I hobbled to the theater to spend my last night at the premiere of a new musical called *Sweeney Todd*. I emerged from the theater trembling. It was pouring, I could barely walk, and the prospect of descending to the Underground having witnessed so many bloody executions didn't thrill me. I could hear my father's outrage if I told him that I had gotten mugged in a subway at eleven o'clock at night. For once, I would shell out a few more dollars—or rather, pounds—and take a cab. I stepped out in traffic and raised my arm. "Taxi!" I shouted. And there I stood, raising my arm and shouting in the rain for half an hour.

Finally, a car with an antenna on the roof pulled up. The kindly man in the passenger seat rolled down his window and said, "Luv, didn't anyone tell you? You can't get a taxi right off the street, especially on a rainy night. We're all on the radio, see?" He held up the receiver. "Where you going, luv? We can squeeze you in before our next call."

Grateful, I slid in the back and named my hotel. The driver maneuvered expertly through the London traffic, and soon we were speeding south across the Thames. "Wait," I said. "My hotel is north of here, not south."

"Shut up," the man ordered. His companion drove faster. I thought of jumping out, but the car didn't slow until we pulled up beside a midnight-black park. The thought crossed my mind that if my kidnappers didn't slash my throat and turn me into a meat pie, I was going to be sexually assaulted for the second time in three weeks, but all they did was demand my wallet. I threw my cash over the seat and jumped out. I tried to run, but my bloodied feet wouldn't take me far. Luckily, my kidnappers sped off, and I was able to find a hotel and rouse a clerk who let me in.

By all rights, I should never have gone anywhere alone again. But waiting in the lobby for the bobbies to show up, I decided that if I didn't want to forego the pleasures of the world—traveling, living in a city, going to the theater—I would need to stop getting taken advantage of. If misfortune did befall me, I couldn't allow whatever happened to shake me up.

The police came and said that fake cabbies often preyed on solitary female tourists. Given that I hadn't taken note of the license, there was little they could do except give me a lift back to my hotel, where I unswaddled my ruined feet, downed a few Tylenol, and vowed to put the disasters of the past few months out of my mind.

In the years that followed, I traveled back and forth across Europe and America, sometimes alone, sometimes in the company of other women. I became a reporter and covered stories that led me to infiltrate a religious cult in New Hampshire and camp out at a Sun Dance on a remote Indian reservation in South Dakota. Last summer, when my partner and I broke up two weeks before the vacation we had been planning, I went anyway and drove around Israel and the West Bank on my own. From time to time, I found myself in precarious situations. But I stayed calm, and nothing ever went so wrong that I couldn't handle it.

I put all those earlier disasters out of my mind. But the mind has ideas of its own. I still suffer flashbacks about big, naked men looming over my bed, and I can't sleep in a room with an air-conditioner or a fan droning in the window. I take my phone to bed, and I warn each new lover there's a high probability that I will, in the throes of a nightmare, clobber him in my sleep. When I told a therapist about the awful summer during which I had been peed on, shot at, and kidnapped, she raised the question of whether I might still be in the throes of post-traumatic stress. "Me?" I said, ticking off all the risky assignments I had covered as a reporter and the faraway destinations to which I had traveled solo, to which the therapist gently replied that this very behavior might constitute its own version of PTSD.

Until recently, I assumed that whatever misfortunes I had experienced that first summer out of college were the result of my own bad choices, even as I read essay after essay in which my female students described the assaults to which so many of them had been subjected—not only rapes, but weird, disturbing shit that never would have happened to a man. Eventually, I was forced to admit that my parents were right—girls *are* more vulnerable to sexual assault than boys. A fake taxi driver isn't likely to target my six-foot-two son as his next patsy. If I had been a male intern at that insurance company, Ron might have resented my good fortune. He might have picked a fight. But I doubt he would have felt the need to humiliate me by breaking into my room and urinating on me. Besides, if a young man did awaken to find a huge, naked drunk guy peeing on him, he would likely punch the intruder in the face and shout: "You asshole, I told you not to drink so many beers!"

That said, the answer isn't learning to shoot a gun. What if I had panicked and shot one of those guys lounging on his stoop in West Philadelphia? Given the choice, I am glad Ron ended up in rehab rather than dead. It was safer to throw my money at those fake cabbies than it would have been to pull a gun and risk having them wrest it from my hand, and far less traumatic than blasting them in their heads and getting spattered by their brains and blood.

What I am advocating isn't target practice, but the kind of self-protective training I gave my son. When Noah was sixteen, he bicycled from Ann Arbor to Detroit, a forty-five-mile trip through some of the most blighted neighborhoods in the country. There he locked his bike to a lamppost, explored the city, then returned to find his mode of transportation stolen. I grounded him for a month—mostly because he had lied about where he was going—but the first time I gave him the keys to my car, he drove right back to Detroit. Rather than ground him again, I accompanied him on his next excursion and showed him where he could park so my car wouldn't get stolen. I bought him a cell phone and urged him to call if he got into trouble. Then I took him on a two-week road trip around Mexico so I could teach him how to travel safely on the cheap.

Would I have done this for a daughter? I doubt it. I probably would have ended up passing along to my daughter a version of the mothering that was passed on to me. Most of Noah's friends' parents were appalled at what I allowed him to do in high school. If he had been a girl, they would have turned me in to social services. As far as I can tell, my female students have been raised in a bizarrely confusing atmosphere in which they are obsessively sheltered and instilled with a vague but overwhelming sense of the terrors that might befall them if they don't check in with their parents every half hour on their cell phones, yet they are led to believe that the world treats men and women equally. Their mothers refrain from sharing their horror stories because they still find those stories so embarrassing, or because they are afraid of giving their own parents cause to say "We told you so," even if those parents no longer are alive, or because they don't want to terrify their daughters out of boldly sallying forth and achieving all they might achieve. Often, the mothers no longer take risks themselves.

I am not saying any of this is easy. Raising a child is like acquiring a priceless vase, then being told that, rather than lock it up, you are supposed to leave it in the street unguarded. But the answer isn't to hover about your kids, terrifying them into leading timid, risk-free lives, nor to pretend that the perils facing young women today aren't (still) more prevalent and insidious than those facing their young male counterparts.

We all know we should do whatever we can to make women's lives safer. In the meantime, we need to teach our daughters that the world does harbor dangers not even the fastest track star can outrun. Of course, if they end up the victim of an assault, we should make sure they get the counseling they need to get back out in the world without being crippled by fear. But what I really hope is that we instill in them a pride that no one instilled in me, a pride that they ventured out there in the combat zone and accomplished what they wanted or needed to accomplish, even without a gun.

RALPH JAMES SAVARESE
Myself on High

She had just won a major literary prize. She was slim, blond, and preposterously attractive. I was slim, blond, and preposterously awkward. Somehow I'd gotten into her poetry writing class as a first-semester freshman. I'd submitted a sonnet about a monk so consumed with sexual longing that he couldn't pray. The monk was me, and the poem, of course, was awful. But because I seemed to know something about formal poetry and because she herself was obsessed with God (the thing my speaker should have been obsessed with), she decided, I guess, to let me in.

Soon I was in love. That her criticism was blunt only fueled in me a certain masochistic tendency. Her comments on poems included "Not fit for a dog's breakfast" and "Grossly sentimental. Try sharing it with your family." I'd walk out of class in a daze. Once, I failed to pause before crossing the street and was nearly workshopped by a bus. The more negative she was, the more determined I became, arranging my words like long-stemmed roses in a vase. The most stubborn of florists, I vowed to win not only her literary regard but also her theological heart.

One day, she announced that she had bought the desk on which a famous twentieth-century poem had been written, and she needed a volunteer to help her husband retrieve it. My hand shot up, and though the word *husband* sounded an alarm, I pictured our future together. "Are you sure you're strong enough to lift it?" she asked in front of everyone.

I would have marched to her house right then, but she told me to come the following Wednesday. When at last I set out, my heart was racing. To calm myself, I hummed the hymn I had sung in church the previous Sunday:

There let the way appear steps unto heav'n;
All that Thou sendest me in mercy giv'n;
Angels to beckon me nearer, my God, to Thee.

As in a dream, the melody seemed to lift me up and deposit me at her door. "John, this is Ralph Savarese," my teacher exclaimed in the front foyer. Shaking her husband's hand, while looking straight at her, I said, "Nice to marry you."

Nice to *marry* you? Before I could process the slip, they were both guffawing. My beloved went down on her knees—she wasn't praying—and pounded the floor. I ducked into a powder room, gasping for air. I wanted to drop the class; I wanted to leave the university; I wanted, in short, to die. The powder room, I belatedly recognized, had no window and thus no escape. The husband had to beg me to come out. "Ralph, it's OK, really. Everyone falls for her," he said, still laughing.

At the end of the course, my poems, too, were humiliated. My teacher told me, "Stop writing. You haven't a lick of talent." But then, three years later, after I had turned to another writer on the faculty and after she had been assigned to read my senior thesis, she took it all back. "You're the only one I've ever been wrong about," she said in a note.

I couldn't believe it. I grabbed that note and ran all over campus, proclaiming my triumph. You'd have thought a DNA test had just cleared a murderer's name. THIS WRITER IS INNOCENT! THIS WRITER HAS A FUTURE! I then went back to my dorm and crafted a reply: at first, a rather effusive thank you, which I scrapped, followed by something uncharacteristically bold. *The only one you've ever been wrong about?* "Don't be so sure," I wrote with liberated fury.

Because she had preached the virtue of brevity, I left it at that—a single jab of the pen. Students who didn't relish proving an authority figure wrong, as I did, or who weren't like mangy, beaten dogs that keep coming back for more would probably have stopped writing after her initial discouragement. Who can say when talent will emerge? What right did anyone have to be so cruel? As I reread my one-liner, I felt a rush of dignity, like a drug injected into my arm. Then fear. What if, at some point, I needed a recommendation from her? "Screw it," I muttered, and sent my reply.

Don't be so sure.

Years later, with my first book of prose coming out, the marketing people begged me to contact her for a blurb. At their request, I had listed all the writers I knew, and they had seized on her. I told them the story of my principled objection, as if to resist, as if to say that I couldn't possibly comply with their request. But the truth was I wanted her to see my book. Of course, I also wanted it to do well, and I knew her name meant something. Plunging headlong into the business of commercial publishing, I repeated to myself what an experienced writer had counseled: "Best not to confuse integrity with self-destruction."

And so I asked my former idol for a blurb—the way one might ask for a favor from the Pope. But would her holiness remember me? Would she be willing to read my book? Although we hadn't kept in touch, I continued to follow her. I knew about her divorce from the man who had coaxed me out of that powder room; I knew that she was teaching at another university; and I knew what sort of reviews she had received after each new book had come out.

"I don't write blurbs anymore," she replied by e-mail. "It takes too much time. You write one and sign my name. No passive voice or clichés." Write one and sign her name? Could I do it? Would it be ethical? What sort of dispensation was this? Behold the stained—yes, stained—glass windows of my soul! And then a voice: "Best not to confuse integrity with self-destruction."

Wavering at first, I attacked the challenge with gusto. Self-encomia poured out of me, as on an assembly line. *Not since Homer has a book had such narrative sweep.* Or: *Only a writer as elegant as F. Scott Fitzgerald could so deftly develop his motifs.* Or—my favorite: *Like that other Italian, Dante Alighieri, Savarese has descended into the underworld and brought back truth itself.* Suddenly, I was nineteen again: I had hair, I was thin, and I craved my teacher's approval, except now I could have it in whatever form I wished.

Imagine praying to God and answering the prayer yourself. Or imagine singing both parts of a love song—say, "Do you love me?" from *Fiddler on the Roof.* "Do you love me?" "Yes, I love you." It was like eating a truckload of Twinkies. The nearly diabetic aftermath left me deflated, even ashamed. I had wanted to be read, I realized; I had wanted to be held in her arms. *Do you read me? Yes, I read you.*

Knowing that I desired her endorsement and offering it precisely as she refused to give it, she mocked the independence I had achieved.

It was a cynical, even malicious, way of honoring a teacher's obligation. I stared at line after line of spurious praise and came to a decision: I wouldn't use a blurb by her. Myself on high? I simply couldn't. Thus, once again I renounced my god. I'd rather be alone, I reasoned, without her.

As I waited for my memoir to be published, I came across books with puffs very much like the ones I had drafted: no passive voice or clichés and lots—I mean lots—of elaborate hyperbole. I understood the temptation. Who doesn't want his book to sell? When mine finally came out, she asked me in an e-mail why I hadn't used her blurb. The publisher had apparently sent her a copy, or she had come across it in a bookstore. "*Your* blurb?" I wanted to say. "*Your* blurb? Is there no limit to your megalomania?" Instead, I thanked her for her generosity and then, breaking free for good, explained that my editor had found it insufficiently flattering.

DANI SHAPIRO
Evil Tongue

1. According to the Talmud, only three sins in Jewish law are so serious they are forbidden under any circumstances, even to save a life. These are murder, idol worship, and adultery. But in many interpretations, there is a fourth sin, equal to, if not worse than, these: *lashon hara*— literally, "evil tongue." It is said of one who is guilty of lashon hara that God declares, "He and I cannot exist in the same world."

2. Here are notes I keep in the back of my old-fashioned Filofax. They are scribbled in an unlikely bright neon pink, in handwriting that looks youthful, moving across the page in buoyantly large loops. I wrote them fifteen years ago, while on the phone with my mother's therapist. *Olga.* I underlined the name twice at the top of the page, as if to express my disbelief that my mother's therapist was calling me. *I read it in one sitting. Gripping, wonderful. I don't think there's anything in there to upset your mother. I think you were not unkind to her. Not at all. In fact, I think you were generous.*

3. Olga was a therapist well known for her work with families. She's probably dead now. She was old, even then. I'll have to look her up. It feels suddenly important to know if she's still out there. Olga had a thick Hungarian accent, and when she said the word generous, it sounded rich, mellifluous, comforting. If my mother's therapist was calling to tell me that my memoir—one I had sneaked to her, in galleys, so that she could prepare my mother for its imminent arrival in bookstores—was not unkind, was in fact generous, not to mention gripping and wonderful, I should take her word for it. Shouldn't I?

4. *In Memoriam.* It's the second listing that comes up in a Google search of Olga's name. She died last year.

5. Olga, even Olga, who is peripheral to this story, a secondary character, and not one who haunts me, is completely identifiable here. If you type *Olga* and *family therapist* into any search engine, there she'll be. The unusual first name. The Hungarian origins. The vaunted reputation in her field. You might come across a video clip in which she described her process as "intuitive," that she believed "the less intervention the better," and that "people should be in charge of their own lives." In truth, I don't think Olga was a good therapist. She was way off-base in her assessment of my mother, who was not a mildly depressed and self-absorbed housewife, one of the "worried well," but rather, had a borderline personality disorder with narcissistic features, which any therapist will tell you is just about the most difficult kind of patient to treat.

Olga was also wrong about my memoir, which, though not cruel, was neither kind nor generous toward my mother. Nor was she remotely on target in her prediction of my mother's response upon reading it. Olga: "I think she'll be fine with it." My mother: "You've ruined my life."

Does my characterization of Olga constitute lashon hara? Would it be more or less so if she were still among us? And have you noticed that I just gave my mother a very unflattering diagnosis? Narcissistic. Borderline. Who am I? Who the hell am I? The daughter. The writer. The one who remains to tell the tale. If she could, my mother would rise from her own grave to tell you these pages are full of lies. I can feel her all around me as I write, the air in my study electric with her silent protest. But in fact, I'm trying to tell the truth here. My version of it, anyway. Trying to tell the truth used to feel like enough.

6. "You shall not go up and down as a tale-bearer among your people." Leviticus 19:16. The Hebrew word for "tale-bearer" is *rakhil,* which has its roots in a word meaning trader or merchant. And when it comes to lashon hara, this bearing of tales is not confined, as you might think, to slander or defamation of character. Truth, lies—it makes no difference. The Talmud tells us that the tongue itself is so dangerous that it must be hidden away behind the protective chamber of the mouth and the teeth, so that it will do no harm.

7. My mother has been dead eight years. My father has been dead twenty-five, more than half my life. There are stories buried with each of them, stories that I can't leave alone. Like a grave-robber, I dig for the bones. Who were my parents? What worlds existed inside them? It's not just simply that I want to know. Or rather, the act of knowing itself is not enough. I assemble the pieces, I fill in the missing ones. I research, extract, remember, imagine. The closest I can ever get to them is by writing. When my pen moves across the page, I am building an edifice, a structure where, before, there was only dust. I am erecting a monument of words, trying to breathe life back into the people I have lost.

8. Rav Yisrael Meir HaKohen—known as the Chafetz Chaim—was a sage considered by Orthodox Jews to be among the thirty-six saints who saved the world. He made a lifelong study of lashon hara, in which he expanded on the idea that death and life are in the power of the tongue. He believed that a pure and sacred tongue—the gift of responsible speech—can elevate the soul, and an irresponsible, wagging tongue can drag a person down to the lowest depths.

9. A few years ago, I received an e-mail from a man I didn't know. He had read my memoir. He had been a close friend of my uncle's and had known my father. He had a story to tell me, a painful, difficult story, he said. He described it as the most shocking thing he'd ever witnessed. Did I want to hear it?

10. The Talmud teaches that "a man should always incite the Good Inclination to battle the evil one" (Berachot 8). According to the Chafetz Chaim, this means that we must always be at war against the Evil Inclination. The Evil Inclination will convince a person that as long as she's telling the truth, it's OK. Perhaps someone deserves to be spoken of maliciously. Maybe it's even a *mitzvah* to reveal a person's misdeeds. But this is lashon hara in its most devious form.

11. Did I want to hear it? Did I? My fingers flew over the keyboard in response. Of course, I wrote to the gentleman who had appeared in my

inbox, an emissary from the world of the dead, I always long to know more about my father. Please, tell me more.

12. The story, the man told me, began in 1962, the year I was born, when my father and his younger brother set out to open a brokerage firm together. My father owned a seat on the New York Stock Exchange, which my grandfather had loaned him the money to buy. They weren't kids, my father and my uncle. My father would have been forty-one, my uncle a few years younger. My uncle, Harvey, found a third partner to join them, a man named Schiffman. The firm was to be called Shapiro Brothers and Schiffman. They rented office space in the Fabrikant Building on West Forty-Seventh Street in Manhattan, in the Diamond District.

13. I feel compelled here to say: I don't know Schiffman. I don't even know if I'm spelling his name correctly. Quite possibly it's Shiffman, or Shiftman. In all likelihood, Schiffman/Shiffman/Shiftman is dead. My father is dead. My Uncle Harvey is dead. Just recently, I wrote again to the man who sent me the e-mail and haven't heard back from him. I fear he may be dead too. The Fabrikants are still a well-known name in the Diamond District, and as far as I know, their only connection to this story is that they rented office space to my father and uncle. Has this yet reached proportions of lashon hara?

14. The day before the bell on the floor of the New York Stock Exchange was scheduled to ring, announcing the opening of Shapiro Brothers and Schiffman, it was discovered that Schiffman had misrepresented himself and couldn't come through with the investment he had promised. Word on the street was that he'd been shady in his business dealings. The bell never rang for Shapiro Brothers and Schiffman. The firm was D.O.A. The rented furniture was hauled away from the office building on Forty-Seventh Street, the assistants fired before their first day on the job. And my grandfather summoned my father and uncle to his apartment on the twenty-seventh floor of The Majestic, on Seventy-Second and Central Park West.

15. I never knew my grandfather. He died when I was nine months old. On a wall in my writing study hangs a black-and-white photograph of him, taken when he was in his fifties. He wears a crisp suit and tie, a yarmulke covering most of his bald head. A pince-nez is clipped to the bridge of his formidable nose. He has a cleft in his chin. It's hard to tell if he's smiling. His gaze is intense. My grandfather was a figure in his world, which is to say the moneyed, Orthodox Jewish world of Manhattan and its environs, which included Israel. He was a textiles magnate, a self-made millionaire, a philanthropist with political ties, a man of influence. When he died suddenly of a heart attack in 1963, the yeshivas in downtown Manhattan and in Brooklyn closed for his funeral. According to a front page obituary in a yellowed, tattered copy of the *Jewish Press*, the block of East Broadway between Allen and Essex was roped off and loudspeakers were placed outside the synagogue so that the assembled crowds could hear the eulogies by the vice-mayor of Tel Aviv, among others, who compared the loss of my grandfather to all of Jewry to that of a Godel B'Yisroel—one of the greats of Israel.

16. The man accompanied my father and Uncle Harvey, he told me in his e-mail, to the apartment at The Majestic, where my grandfather was waiting for them. He described the grand formal living room with its sweeping view of Central Park, the trees, horses, and carriages, pedestrians reduced to the size of Monopoly pieces. A room I know well. My grandmother had a stroke at my grandfather's funeral, from which she never recovered, and she lived in that apartment on Central Park West, cared for by two aides, for all the years of my childhood. When I was in college, I used to crash there when I was in the city with my friends, after partying too much.

On the day of the summons, my grandmother stood silently next to my grandfather, who began screaming at his two sons the moment they walked through the door and into the marble foyer. They did not remove their coats, but stood in the entrance to the living room with their hats in their hands. My father was pale. My uncle shook violently. For half an hour, my grandfather tore into them relentlessly in a manner—so said the now-probably-dead man—that was the most vicious display of emotional violence he had ever seen in his life. At the end of it, they turned—my father, my uncle, their friend—and left the apartment without having uttered a word.

17. Recently, at a dentist appointment, my dentist peered into my mouth with great interest. "You have something there called *linea alba*," he said. "It's a white line on either side of your tongue. It's unusual, but not a cause for concern—you must be biting your tongue in your sleep."

18. I have kept the yellowed newspaper clippings about my grandfather, the tributes, the letters of praise. The outpouring of sorrow over his death. I have felt, somehow, that being his granddaughter accorded me a certain safety. Unlike my mother's father, an immigrant chicken farmer who died many years before I was born, my paternal grandfather was someone who had carved a permanent place for himself on the sides of buildings, on plaques in auditoriums. A great man. Everybody said so. The Yiddish word *yichus* means "pedigree," "good blood," or "well born." But dig deeper, and the more subtle meaning emerges: to have yichus, one must live up to the promise of one's family's stature.

19. According to Rabbi Moses M. Yoshor, whose seminal biography of the Chafetz Chaim was first published in Yiddish in 1937, there is a basic principle in medicine that a discolored, unclean tongue is a symptom of some abnormal, disturbed condition of the body—the physical state. This is also true in spiritual dimensions. A tongue that is "discolored" and unclean is an indication that the internal system of the person's spirit is not functioning properly.

20. Uncle Harvey and his wife divorced when I was thirteen, but she remained in my life, and shortly after hearing the story of Shapiro Brothers and Schiffman from my e-mail interlocutor, I met her for coffee in New York. Ruth is in her late seventies and very hard of hearing. Once we settled into a quiet corner table of a café on the Upper West Side, not far from where my grandparents had lived, I told her about the unexpected e-mail and my discovery of the story

I assumed she already knew: the deceit, the closing of the firm before it ever opened, my grandfather's fury. But when I got to the part about my father and Harvey being summoned to a meeting in my grandparents' apartment, she stopped me, mystified. Her sound amplifier rested on the table between us, as if it were a translating device. "What meeting? I don't know anything about a meeting."

21. When my first memoir (indeed, I have written more than one) was published, an aunt and a few cousins never really spoke to me again. An uncle called to let me know that I had misspelled his third wife's name and asked if it was possible to insert errata. Many relatives politely averted their gaze, as if having stumbled into an occupied bathroom by mistake. Still others were gracious and unerringly kind. But my mother? As has already been established, Olga, my mother's therapist, thought my mother would find my book generous and—what was it? Oh, yes. Gripping and wonderful. Olga did not foresee that my memoir would become, for many of the people in my mother's life, a *Cliff's Notes* of sorts. I couldn't have imagined it myself. *Oh, the daughter has written a memoir?* Everyone in her world—from her doorman to her accountant—read my book in an attempt to figure her out.

22. A famous Chasidic fable illustrates the gravity of lashon hara: a man went around his village gossiping and telling all manner of stories, with no concern about the impact of his behavior. But in time, he began to realize that his stories had hurt people, and he felt remorseful. He paid a visit to his rabbi, and asked how he could make amends. Take a feather pillow, the rabbi told him, cut it open, and spread the feathers to the wind. Simple enough. The man did as the rabbi bade him. He came back for further instructions. Now, said the rabbi, go out and collect all of the feathers and return them to the pillow. Ashamed, and without even a handful of feathers, the man returned to the rabbi once more. Your words are like feathers, the rabbi told him. Once they leave your mouth, you know not where they will go, and you can never retrieve them again.

23. As I told my aunt the story of the meeting—the screaming old man, the silent sons—her eyes filled with tears. Decades peeled away, as if the layers of a fruit, leaving only the exposed and tender core. I could see the young wife and mother she had been. Her sad, unhappy marriage. Her bitter, contentious divorce. Her fragility and shame. Her four children devastated by the shattering of their home. "That makes sense." Her voice trembled. "I've never understood. But finally it makes sense." "What?" I asked her. Something powerful was happening. I had no idea what was going on. "That night." The words tumbled out. "Harvey tried to kill himself that night."

24. I am a tale-bearer among my people. Rakhil—a trader, a merchant. Would it be fair to say that I'm profiting from this tale? Why the words, the endless stream of words? What if I were to tell you that the pieces of my history are jagged and sharp. Those pieces—left alone—will shred me to bits. What if I were to tell you that in assembling them I am traveling backward through time: my mother is not crazy, my father is not depressed, my aunt isn't fragile, my uncle not suicidal. My grandfather opens his arms in an embrace of his two sons. Everyone is still alive. The story—if it is a story—always contains within it the chance of another ending.

25. That night was Uncle Harvey's first suicide attempt, though it wouldn't be his last. "Harvey was never the same after that," my e-mail correspondent had written to me. "How different it might have been if his father had, instead, comforted him and offered words of support?" My grandfather never told my Aunt Ruth about the events that had taken place earlier that night. If he considered his role in what happened, he kept it to himself. Instead, he blamed her for her husband's overpowering despair, and told her she'd better figure out how to be a better wife.

26. My grandfather was the man eulogized as a Godel B'Yisroel. The man who never missed a morning *minyan*. Who recited from the *sefer Tehillim* every morning of his life. The man whose death inspired a member of Israel's Parliament to write, in a letter of condolence to my

grandmother, that he was heartbroken and completely bewildered, that generations upon generations would be the beneficiaries of his good deeds. Yet he was the man who so violently berated his sons that it had caused one of them to make an attempt on his own life. The man who did not take responsibility for his own actions. Who allowed a fragile woman to spend most of her life believing her own culpability. He was all these things.

27. "What right do you have?" my mother used to yell at me. "How dare you?" She is here now. They all are. In my writing study, they crowd around me. Their photographs hang askew on the walls. "Tell this," they say. "Don't tell that." Who are you—daughter, granddaughter, niece, cousin, wife, mother, friend, witness, bystander—the one who became the writer, the tale-bearer, the one who lays the pieces on the floor like a mosaic, a puzzle, a path through her own wilderness. The one who gets the last word. Who are you to tell our stories?

28. *Yizkor*—one of the most sacred prayers in the liturgy—means "to remember." The Jewish people don't believe in heaven or hell, but we do believe that our souls live on through memory. *He of blessed memory. May his memory be a blessing.* This is the language most often used about our dead. So perhaps I should leave this story alone, to exist only as a brief e-mail correspondence between an old man and a writer. After all, my grandfather was a true patriarch, Abraham to a tribe of more than forty great-grandchildren, including my own son. I am telling a tale about a dead man, told to me by a dead man. At the same time, I am holding yellowed clippings, so soft with age that the paper may crumble in my hands. Is it possible that this isn't lashon hara, but my own form of Yizkor, of honoring the dead?

29. I went to see my dentist again. He peered into my mouth with even greater interest. With a piece of gauze, he held my tongue between his fingers, and pulled. He pressed a small mirrored instrument against the insides of both my cheeks, examining the linea alba. He was silent as he removed the instrument and made a note in my chart. "It's gotten a bit worse, but don't worry," he finally said. "We see all sorts of things on

the tongue. We'll keep an eye on it. You have one of those mouths that needs to be watched."

MARK SLOUKA
The Academy of Sciences

There are times I think the past is nothing more than a room attached to ours. We enter it a hundred times a day, argue with whoever's there; we flatten a cowlick, move the vase, true the picture on the wall.

I was looking out at the garden the other day (something I tend to do in November) when I thought of my father. For just one second it seemed impossible that he should be eighty-nine and living in Prague—where they were having an early winter, he said—while I found myself six time zones back, renting a house no more than five minutes from where we'd once lived as a family. It felt like I could just walk over, find us there.

A cat appeared on the fence and a gust of sparrows rose against the neighbor's house. I'd cleared the beds the day before, hauling off long armloads of pea vines segmented like the legs of sea creatures; for the first time in months I could see the wooden borders framing the dirt.

Zdenek Slouka. When I say my father's name out loud, I hear his voice coming out of my mouth. Years ago I stopped using my middle name— his first. He never mentioned it. He's remarried now, but it doesn't matter: we're the only ones left, and we both know it.

It's hard for me to see his life as anything but a column of subtractions, as if God, picking flowers for the celestial vase, decided out of curiosity to pluck one bare—he loves me, he loves me not. His parents, whom he had to leave behind when he escaped from Czechoslovakia in 1948, died before the regime that had exiled him fell. He never saw them again; I never met them. His sister, Luba, my only aunt, threw herself out of a window in 1950, though my father wouldn't know about it for two years, imagining her all that time walking to school or lying in the grass above the athletic stadium in Brno with her friends—a temporary afterlife, like an image in a bubble. When a letter finally got through in September of 1952, the knowledge that she'd been gone so long made for a grief both slightly uncanny and tinged by insincerity—like going under anesthesia, I imagine, watching your own leg being removed.

And so it went, petal by petal. An old friend, a Latinist reduced to doing manual labor for refusing to join the Party, sat down to dinner the day before Christmas 1966, cracked a walnut, and died. Eventually there were just the three of us: my father, my mother, and me. The nuclear unit, famously unstable.

Whatever the question, my mother, whom he must have made love with at least once, was not the answer. An only child herself (capable of the most spontaneous joy I've ever known in an adult), she was broken by fifty, battered by gusts of sadness and rage. When she finally divorced my father in 1991 after forty-three years of marriage, she moved, along with the uncomfortable suburban furniture that had filled our home, to a mold-ridden farmhouse in Moravia where she re-created the rooms she'd been so miserable in, then gradually forgot everything: our cabin at Lost Lake, the days we laughed, the hot afternoons at the station when we'd wait for my father in the burnt electric smell of the ties and the steel—everything. A mercy for someone infatuated with regret. "Zdenek? Zdenek who?" she asked me, the last time I saw her, still here but not.

Which left just my father and me to carry all that history. We carried it well enough—my father especially. Wedded to reason, inclined like a heliotrope to whatever could be known (author of the monograph *The Intercontinental Shelf and International Law*), he had the gift of being able to accept the gavel coming down, of being able to bear the sentence: "It wasn't." The comma and the conjunction he left to me, the lord of revision: "It wasn't, but it could have been."

"It could have been." He must have sensed the gene in me long before I did. There I was, like an apprentice St. Sebastian, inserting my baby arrows into my skin, practicing. My mother's son. Time didn't lay down its tracks in a line for me, the print didn't set: I mourned every house before we left it, then refused to leave it after we did. *Was* meant nothing to me; long before I knew what the conditional mood was, I was humming its tune: *If he had known, if she had said, if we had stayed.* My life, my work, was one long argument for commutation.

My father had no ear for it. To traffic in "if" was absurd, an exercise in masochism. What was, was. His sister was gone, sent in a fit of delirium tremens on an errand through thin-paned glass to the courtyard three stories below. His mother, awakened by a sound she would never forget, was also gone. It was the way it was.

In December 1948, the day he learned that he was to be arrested, my father quietly began making arrangements to escape his own country. It couldn't have been easy—he could tell no one. Those who knew him would be interrogated; their ignorance would need the ring of truth. He'd have to vanish with a wink and a wave, disappear from their lives like a magician's assistant stepping into a wardrobe. The only thing making it bearable—a saving irony—was his certainty that he wouldn't be gone long: a year, maybe two. The regime could never last. He was twenty-five years old.

The afternoon before he left, my father told his mother and sister that he'd be going to see a friend in Prague after the late edition of the paper. He'd be back in Brno on Monday. He gave his mother a quick hug, careful not to raise her suspicions, kissed his sister on the forehead. His father was still at the office.

At eight o'clock that night my father walked out of the clatter and ring of carriage returns for a few minutes to wake himself up in the cold winter air and ran into his father coming home from work. The two men stopped to talk as the snow came down. He was going to Prague for a day or so, my father said.

He'd heard, my grandfather said, lighting a cigarette. Did he have everything he needed?

It was an odd question. Sure, my father said. He'd be staying with Mirek.

"Money?"

He was fine, my father said.

My grandfather nodded, then looked up the street at the cones of snow coming down from the lamps like light in a comic book. "So," he said, "I better be getting home, before your mother begins to wonder." He smiled (and I can imagine that smile, though fifty years have passed since he died, because I'm only two years younger than he was then): "You'd better get back in there—don't you have a newspaper to put out?" And he put out his hand and my father took it, and then he was walking away up the sidewalk past the closed shops toward the square.

My father stood there until he couldn't see him any longer and went back inside. He would never see him again. He'd be sixty-eight before he returned, his own son ten years older than he'd been when he left.

The day he told me about that evening we were sitting on the deck behind our house. Things had happened the way they did, he said, imparting the lesson, the attitude, as always. What was, was. So what if he'd known, if he'd held his father's hand a little longer, or given him a hug—he hadn't. He looked out over our yard, already figuring out what needed his attention. He could use my help in the garden.

It was 1978, summer. I was home from college. We were still a family. My mother still had a memory.

Seventeen years later saw some changes. The revolution had swept in like a welcome tide, receded; the three of us had separated. My mother had returned to Moravia. My father was living in Prague by then, working in the Academy of Sciences on Narodni Street, a cavernous, museumlike building with forty-foot ceilings and empty, unlit corridors. He'd stay late, working, reading, drinking, and I'd find him there, groping my way toward the flat European switches on the wall that lit another section of hallway, temporarily, then went out behind me.

It was there, in the Academy of Sciences building, my father told me, that he experienced one of the oddest moments of his life.

He'd been working late, he said, when a knock on the door nearly stopped his heart. It was well after midnight; the building had been dark for five hours or more. My father opened the door to a man in his early forties carrying a small, battered briefcase. The man extended his hand and gave his name—the standard Czech greeting. "Zdenek Slouka," he said.

My father, naturally enough after all the years he'd lived in America, assumed the man had asked him his name instead of giving his own. "I'm Zdenek Slouka," he replied, "can I help you?" The man smiled—a kind, strangely familiar smile. "No, I know you're Zdenek Slouka," he said. "The thing is, so am I."

They talked nearly till dawn, and a story emerged—a story, my father said, that he would never have believed if he hadn't heard it himself. The other Zdenek Slouka had been conceived out of wedlock. He didn't remember his father, a man from Brno, who had quietly supported him through his childhood and who had asked, in return, that he be named Zdenek.

One by one, the pieces locked into place. The conclusion was obvious. The other Zdenek, my father told me, was from the same logging town that his father had originally come from, and to which he'd begun returning late in life. It was there that he'd had an affair, fathered a December child. And it was there, apparently, staggering under the erasure of his family—his daughter's suicide, his wife's slide into madness, his son's disappearance into exile—that he'd taken a stab at the impossible, a gesture at once absurd and bottomlessly sad. He began again. He fathered a son, then named him after the one he'd lost. The man in the office was not just his namesake, my father said, but his half-brother. In other words, my uncle.

We were sitting in a café on Londynska street. My father signaled the waitress and pointed to his vodka. Of course the whole thing was mad, a testament to the things that pain can drive us to, no more. But the man was real enough. And it was a comfort, wasn't it?— knowing we had a relation in the world, a good man apparently, eager to know us both.

I lived with the thought of this man, this second father, for quite a few years. Although I never actually met him—he was always gone, or traveling, when I visited Prague—I'd hear about him from my father. He called from Vienna, he'd tell me; he was coming to town the week after next. Over time, I heard less, forgot to ask. Gradually he faded, a photograph left in the development tray. It didn't matter. Fixed in my imagination, having elbowed a space for himself in the past, he lived on. It took a long time for me to admit that he'd probably never been.

It was the small things that turned the key: a date that didn't match, a part that didn't fit, even that overelaborate frame in which the thing had been set: the fateful knock at midnight, the long-lost brother, emerging from the dark...My father had been drinking then, weighing accounts. I can see him, sitting up late in the Academy of

Sciences, working his way down the bottle. The rationalist, cornered at last. His own losses he could bear; my own—imagined or real—were another thing. I was his only son, the only child of only children—existentially alone in terms of blood—and he was getting old.

So he made me a gift. His father, forced to let his son go into the world alone, had had no choice. He did. I'd have a relation, a companion—someone to talk to in the long years of exile.

Regrets accrue, old investments come to term; I've never been able to laugh at the concessions that love can force from us.

But I don't think it was for me alone that my father bent his faith, that he tried, awkwardly, to walk into the past, to flatten a cowlick, adjust the vase, make it right; there was another consideration, a moment in the past, like a bone in the throat, that needed his attention. And I know what it was because now and then time leaves a marker—a note in the margin, a corner turned down—so that we know where to look.

December 1948. It's snowing. They talk. My grandfather knows. He turns, walking quickly, the years lowering like an anvil. Fifty years later my father, unable to bear it, comes to his rescue: he stalls the descent, jams a story between iron and stone, delivers to him a second son.

XU XI
My Mother's Story: The Fiction & Fact

First in a series of essays called, collectively, My Mother's Story.

My mother, Kathleen Klin Phoa (潘吉林) circa 1948. Fact.

A student at St. Mary's Canossian secondary school in Kowloon, Hong Kong. Fact.

Despite the hiatus that was the war, she was still a girl. Oh, she knew she was almost a woman, but inside, she felt like the schoolgirl she still was who had to matriculate, to further her studies, to become a medical doctor. That was the plan in the run up to 1947.

By then, the Japanese had left Singapore and she must have wondered what the Convent of the Holy Infant Jesus, her former boarding school, looked like now. She had gone home to Indonesia when the war began, but her father had sent the family to the hills of Wonosobo in Central Java, away from the occupation. In Tjilatjap, their family home was gone, leveled by the bombs, as she would tell us all through our childhood, when she was still "Mum," long before that got lost to Alzheimer's. Her version of the war in Indonesia may be fiction, but we have the documents to prove she did indeed attend the Singaporean convent school, and that she later did attend St. Mary's Canossian in Hong Kong from where she did indeed matriculate, and that the University of Hong Kong did indeed offer her a place to study. Medicine is another story—she never attended university. She qualified as a pharmacist instead and either apprenticed or worked for a brief while at Queen Mary Hospital. Then she met Dad, got pregnant, and became "Mum," and could no longer be a girl.

But in 1947, well before she met Dad in Hong Kong, she was, perhaps, already too old to be a girl.

It already feels like summer even though it's only May. It is 2011 and my mother and I are in a taxi on the way to her regular medical checkup. Dr. Pei is a geriatric specialist; over half a year ago, her Malaysian GP recommended specialized elder care. Her GP, Raymond, I've known for years as the author of a memoir, because we once shared the same publisher. He became our choice when Mum first needed medical supervision after a lifetime without a regular doctor. He's my doctor now as well, since I moved back to Hong Kong in early 2010 to a full-time university position to help my sister with Mum's Alzheimer's care. This return "home" was after a dozen or so years of a freelance life, inhabiting the flight path connecting New York, Hong Kong, and the South Island of New Zealand, though New York was home then. A life I miss.

That's Kowloon Tong Club, she says. *And Maryknoll School. And St. Teresa's Church.* Yes, yes, yes, I say as I do each time she exclaims at these passing landmarks, as if these were sightings after a long time away. Perhaps for her they are. She and Dad held their wedding reception at the club, just as I did for my first marriage. *Champagne flowed,* but that's Dad's story, not hers, for both weddings, theirs and mine. She sewed her own white dress—more cream than white—which doubled as her evening gown to fit an eighteen-inch waistline. Except that's fiction, because by the time they married, her waist could no longer have been eighteen inches, assuming it ever was, but that is my mother's story and has been ever since she heard Vivien Leigh utter that svelte ideal in *Gone with the Wind,* one of the few movies she ever recalls.

We "the children"—as we forever were to our parents, and even to ourselves—shredded that dress in play over the years and now, none of the dresses she sewed remains, except for one Thai silk cocktail dress. It's black with a pattern of large golden blooms, less garish than you might imagine, with a shawl of the same material. When I unearthed it while clearing out the horrifying accumulation her home had become in the nine years after Dad's death, no one was sure whether

Mum or her older sister Caroline sewed it, or if it even belonged to her. But there it was, never worn, and I kept it thinking it could be taken in to fit me. Five years later, I'm still thinking. Recently, I tried on a dress that was almost a dead ringer for one my mother taught me to sew when I was a teenager. Brown-and-blue batik shaped from a Simplicity sheath pattern, to flatter a *cheongsam*-perfect figure—just slender enough for that high-necked, tight, Sino dress-glove—the most Chinese thing about me.

Pure Chinese, my mother declared of her *wah kiu* Indonesian ancestors in Tjilatjap. The *wah kiu* or "overseas Chinese" of Southeast Asia were more Chinese than the ones left behind on the Mainland, even after five generations, their purity preserved by racist distaste for dark-skinned Indonesian natives. Mum was not inclined to reflect on the wrongs and rights of racism. It was simply pride, pride in the family she left behind to pursue a girl's ambitions in Hong Kong. And yet. *Cuckoo! They were all cuckoo,* she would exclaim, when telling family tales of her inbred cousins, nieces, nephews, in-laws, the irony of this racial "purity" completely lost on her. Like her memory now. *Cuckoo.*

Don't get so dark—you'll be ugly, she yelled at me and my second sister, for as long as she could be Mum, in charge of herself and us, for as long as she could deny us our Indonesian bloodline and pigmentation. *Pure Chinese,* unlike my father's mixed-race heritage. Our dark skin was Dad's fault, not hers, of that she made sure we knew.

She got pregnant in 1953 and gave birth to me exactly nine months and sixteen days after her wedding, just-in-virginal-enough time. *I'll bring you the moon and the stars if you'll marry me* is what the girl fell in love with, but the woman muttered over a lifetime of bitterness about *men(!) sex(!) prostitutes(!) geishas(!) concubines(!)* loud enough for all her girls to hear, for all her girls to doubt future declarations of love, despite our inbred susceptibility to same.

The problem, I believe, was the elongation of her girlhood.

In 1947, at the age of twenty-seven, my mother was too old for school. This is probably fact. What is also more than likely a fact is that she (and later, Aunt Caroline) adjusted her legal age upon arrival in Hong Kong by shaving off four years. When you've heard a story all your life, it becomes fact even if it's fiction. Especially true here when I cannot verify anything from Indonesian birth certificates that, in any case, appear not to exist or have vanished from my mother's papers. What does exist is my mother's Hong Kong identity card with the birth year 1924.

Power of attorney for an aging and confused Mum is a curious thing. We the children are "responsible" for the feeding and care of a woman who was nothing if not responsible for everything about our family, even when that responsibility was no longer required and had become an annoyance to us, the children. Squatting on my mother's rooftop, in a former guest room converted into that British horror, the bedsit, I am now the "responsible" adult-girl in this home, as my mother once was for me.

Because girls are not responsible for anyone other than themselves, which, I suspect, we pretend to believe, my mother and sisters and I. *Heavy, so heavy,* my sister whispers, stooping her shoulders for our imaginary burden, as together, we watch Mum age.

> *I flip when a fellow sends me flowers*
> *I drool over dresses made of lace…*
>
> *I'm strictly a female female*
> *And my future I hope will be*
> *In the home of a brave and free male*
> *Who'll enjoy being a guy having a girl like me.*
>
> —from "I Enjoy Being a Girl" in the musical *The Flower Drum Song*
> Lyrics: Oscar Hammerstein Music: Richard Rodgers

It was fun being a girl. At nineteen, when she came home after finishing Senior Cambridge in Singapore, she was still her Daddy's girl, the "flower of Tjila," a talented tennis player and the one the other girls envied, the one all the boys chased. Meanwhile, her brothers were here and there, she claimed, helping to run Daddy's stevedore operation at home in the village, preening in their sharkskin suits while flunking out of school, and generally frittering away the family money.

That could be fiction but it has the ring of truth. The sisters, however, were becoming nuns or marrying and popping out babies, and the one who married the homosexual and didn't consummate her marriage had at least married money and could afford to adopt.

She and Caroline did not have to marry, not yet. They were still girls running wild and free, and she the smarter and younger and prettier by far. A girl can dream about becoming a doctor before the grind of medical school is reality. A girl can make plans to shore up her science and math for when summer days are over and the academic year begins anew up north in Hong Kong. It was always summer in Indonesia, though, where the food was rich and fatty, yummy and fatty, around-the-clock plentiful and fatty, since everything is fried in palm oil. Breakfast served at dawn, snacks at eleven, lunch at one, tea later in the afternoon, dinner at seven or eight, snacks at night before bed. Daily. Her mother had eleven children and ran a household of servants who cooked and cooked and cooked. And then she died of diabetes, or so we think, since we can't be sure if it was that or cancer (which several of our aunts and uncles had) or both, the result of a diet of wealth instead of health and common sense.

But unlike her mother, Mum was not illiterate, this ambitious girl who dreamt of higher learning.

Meanwhile, she enjoyed being a girl.

Eight years later, two years after Japanese hostilities in Southeast Asia subsided, she was still, unfortunately, a girl. And she was probably twenty-seven. And not a doctor. And not yet even a wife.

Even in the twenty-first century, mutton does not pass for lamb, regardless of Hollywood nip-tucks, just as décolletage fails on skinny women as leggings do on the fat. A smart girl can memorize formulas and skeletal parts and cram for exams. A determined girl can force aside fears to head out alone, on board a ship bound for Hong Kong, where she must make her own way without family or friends. An outgoing girl can rely on personality to win friends and influence people. A tough girl can endure winters in a subtropical climate when all she has ever known are the tropics. A pretty girl can smile at men who continue to fall at her feet.

But a woman is a woman growing older, even if she thinks she's still a girl.

Here it is, 2011, and I am, unfortunately, no longer a girl, though I am not yet a woman growing quite as old as my mother. My life is on hold the way Mum's was when war raged and her education was postponed. I think she had more fun, though she may have paid more harshly for it later. I had a life once, I sometimes say now, one that trod a path less trodden, a path that was mine. But then it forked away, like memory.

So there it was, 1947, and my mother was either twenty-three or twenty-seven, getting the best marks she could. *An A in Math! My male teacher said I was the smartest student!* Did she prettify and flirt, seducing with her womanly form? Or was it nose in books, the grindstone wearing away time, time, time?

In the report cards we found, there was indeed always an A in Math; she neglected to mention the Cs in other subjects, like music and history. *You can do Math if you try!* she shouted at my baby sister, then aged around seven or eight, as I tried to help her with arithmetic, not her strong suit ever. But that sister did eventually pass all her public exams in math and got an Ivy League PhD in criminology. One day, to her own horror, she even taught college-level statistics for social science research.

But a favorite child is lost without Daddy to confer that favoritism.

A handsome suitor who adores you confers the favoring, even if somewhere deep inside, suspicion rankles. A potential mate from the right background, even if it's not quite as good as your own, likely engenders *he'll do, he'll do, he promised me the moon and the stars,* even if this is something you don't say aloud.

I have tried to write fiction of their meeting. It fails every time. The romance of my parents' love—because I must believe that they were once in love—has lost its girlish innocence. In the womb of Mum's bridal gown and fancy shoes, amid the rhinestones and perfume we rummaged through as children, my parents could *only* be in love. Dad was handsome, Mum was beautiful. The faded photos and our memories do not lie. Many years later, long after the engagement diamond and marriage and children, long after my father's near-bankruptcy and philandering, long after Mum's tumble down the boulevard of shattered dreams, Dad bought her a diamond to replace the one she sold, along with all her other jewelry, to feed us when we were broke. It was large, not especially beautiful, and she wore it for a while and then removed it. Despite her bourgeois upbringing, despite all her carping about money till we the children drowned her out, despite, despite, despite, despite it all, what she wanted most was love, not things. She taught us that well, even as she gave us diamonds and gold as insurance against disaster. *You can run with gold,* she repeated through our childhood, as if we, too, would one day have to hide our valuables because the fill-in-the-blank military might descend upon her adopted city, Hong Kong, and we, too, would have to sail away, run for the hills, or find a seat on the last flight out of Shanghai for Hong Kong, as Dad did in 1949. That was the wrong year for a young Chinese Indonesian guy to be a student at St. John's University, playing the violin and saxophone in his spare time, extolling the pleasures of the capitalist's dream life when the Communists came to roost.

    I sold my diamond necklace back to Mum when I was in my early thirties. My then-second-now-ex-husband, a jazz musician, and I needed food, shelter, drugs, and drink more than bling. I threatened to sell it, and she finally relented and gave me the cash I needed in exchange for her gift. *Never look a gift horse*...but I did.

It is 2011 and life is lonely in "the squat." The man who has loved me for the past fourteen years, and been my friend even longer, is back "home" in New York. We e-mail, we Skype. We christen the bedsit the squat. I fly back whenever I can, en route to conferences, in between work. My mother met him a long time ago, back when she still was Mum. Sometimes, I mention his name, and this, strangely, she seems to recognize, even though she's rarely seen him. He continues to love me, despite, despite, despite.

    And for those brief times we're together, this fellow brings me flowers.

My girlhood was filled with cheap romance. Champagne flowed while the guests danced downstairs in our penthouse flat, the one with a view of the Hong Kong harbor. Another fact. I used to imagine other harbors from up high—Rio de Janeiro, San Francisco, Monaco because Grace Kelly was a princess. A beautiful life. But Mum could have done with something else—the moon and the stars perhaps—because a life is only beautiful if you are.

When did he turn away from her beauty?

I remember the Japanese woman in her kimono. She was young (they always are, aren't they, the eye candy of men who stray). More important, she was gentle and sweet, probably bright, but this could be my fiction of remembrance. The niece of my father's business associate. When Dad died, we the children had to sort through dozens of loose photos of strangers. There were several in Japan, very few included Mum, and what remains is the memory of her broken-record voice, *your dad wanted to take a second wife, a Japanese geisha! I said, then I'll divorce you,* over and over and over again, until we stopped listening, stopped caring, stopped arguing the illogic of her declaration, since part of the point of being a geisha is *not* to marry. Mostly. Besides, I'm not so sure Dad ever visited a geisha, because a hostess who serves drinks—the stuff of those photos—is not necessarily a geisha. He did go to Japan, sometimes for weeks at a time, until the business collapsed and the trips stopped, his T-Bird taken away. I was ten.

Dad never took a second wife—which was legal in Hong Kong till the mid-sixties. He simply tuned out his first one over time. Mum never did get a divorce, not even after that bout of the clap when she was older, much too old, really, to suffer such slings and arrows. By then I had long been defending her against Dad, since this oldest child was always the one, the *only* one who could argue with him, being Daddy's favored daughter, at least when I was still a girl. Despite being my mother's least favored child and lifelong nemesis, even I knew when my talent ought to be used—that verbal ability she so despised—despite my unconditional love for Dad, and the conditional one for her.

Somewhere along the way, Mum the girl stopped flipping and drooling. Somewhere along the way, she became Mum the woman.

Was it when I got tonsillitis and had to be hospitalized for the operation, or when my sister tumbled off the slide at school and sported a gigantic bruise on her forehead? Or when she had to fire my youngest sister's baby *amah*, the nanny, because she was *dirty, so dirty, she didn't wash your sister properly and she got a rash all over her bottom!* When Mum flipped, it was to shout at servants, sometimes at us, and most of all to complain about Dad. Until my brother was born.

Things changed with the boy, the one and only boy. My father was not unusually boy-crazy at the expense of his daughters, the way so many Asian fathers still are, but the boy-at-last *is* cause for excitement, even among us girls. For my mother, it was her female-female moment. My brother had asthma and needed the special care that her pharmaceutical training helped to provide. Now, at last, she had a raison d'etre as a woman.

Chinese motherhood is a social-climbing affair. Having delivered the boy, at last, she could relax. Oh, she was *such* a girl! Behind closed doors she would say of all those aunties married to uncles who were part of our parents' circle, *only a secretary, that's all she is, none of Mum's daughters will be secretaries…*or flight attendants or nurses. No, we girls would be the CEO, the pilot, or the doctor—so Mum decreed. And yet, there she was, playing house with Daddy, having given up her own profession as a pharmacist, because a well-kept wife is the ultimate sign of success. Better than the woman who has to work.

A harsh downslide when she returned to work because my father was broke. She did it, though, and could still brag of being a professional, not *only a secretary,* because only *she* could sign for the "dangerous drugs" at the pharmacies and pharmaceutical manufacturers that employed her. She was happier then, an almost-woman then.

In 2011, "second wives village" in Shenzhen is already old news in Hong Kong. Since concubinage has long been criminalized, Chinese men cross the border to the Mainland where a factory girl or karaoke hostess or hardworking rural miss will "marry" the one who can set her up to play house. *Pretty Woman* is fiction. The fact is all the pretty girls trade their faces for their fates. All she need do is have the boy to assure her husband of his virility. That the Communist Party once placed women alongside men as equals—in the factories, on the farms, to fight in the military—feels like ancient history.

With a pound and a half of cream upon my face.
—"I Enjoy Being a Girl"

But Mum was educated. Mum was modern. She was proud of what she achieved, this girl who would be queen, *independent,* the way she urged us all to be. *Girls need to be educated,* she told us all through our noisy childhood, *in case their husbands can't support them.* Girls, not women. Girls who won't grow up.

Your daddy wouldn't let me work when we got married. He insisted I give up my job. Over and over and over again through our noisy, noisy childhood of messages and media that did not match until we stopped listening. The girl who would be queen could not shed the princess brat who wanted it all.

Yet it was as Woman and Mother that she finally found her face.

It is 2011 and I am much too conscious of my conditional love for Mum. This is me being rebel girl, the one who must tear down every social construct her mother holds dear, the girl who is still the daughter trying to prove herself better than her mother. Meanwhile, Mum is old and has slid into the "moderate to severe" stage of Alzheimer's. That much is fact.

It is 2011 and the harsh heat of Hong Kong is finally moderating with November. At our last doctor's visit, I tell him my mother's latest story. That she asks to go home to Tsimshatsui because she is time-wandering back to our home in the sixties and doesn't realize she *is* home; that she thinks it's time to go to work; that her memory for faces is slipping because she did not really recognize our visiting Seattle cousin whom she recognized only a year earlier. That she took a fall recently, bruising her shoulder. It happened on the veranda when she went out and must have been bending down, I say, probably to check the potted plants, and lost her balance. *Were there witnesses to the fall?* he asks and I say no because our domestic helper was in the kitchen at the time and I wasn't there. So her green encounter may be fiction because I like to remember the flowers my mother planted, the orchids that graced the veranda of our childhood, the mini orange trees she brought into our home at Chinese New Year. Her green thumb that kept her rooted to the soil in this harsh city of her womanhood, where the *best years of her life* were stolen by the cheap romance of being a girl.

It is 2011 and Mum is dying.

It is 2011 and I am trying to be a woman, not a girl, for the mother who would be queen.

ABOUT PATRICIA HAMPL
A Profile by Jennifer Brice

By the end of her thirties, Patricia Hampl had published two poetry collections and a critically acclaimed memoir. When a radio interviewer asked her what was next, she replied airily, "I have it in mind to work on fiction from now on." What happened in the following years just goes to show that writers are no more adept than anyone else at predicting their futures.

Since her first memoir, *A Romantic Education,* Hampl has published four more works of nonfiction—three memoirs and an essay collection on memory and imagination—as well as a "fantasia" on the Czech composer Antonín Dvořák's 1893 visit to Iowa. Although her work is widely read, Patricia Hampl is also a writer's writer—lyric, cerebral, a boon companion at any stage of the writer's journey. The arc of her career parallels the rise of personal writing in America in the past half-century. It may be that the genre most closely associated with memory—"that captivating mystery," she calls it—chose her, not the other way around. Indeed, she uses the language of surrender to describe her writing process. "I conscripted myself to be the protagonist of these books," she told National Public Radio's Diane Rehm in 2007. "As memoir began gaining ground, I realized I was riding this strange tiger."

Because the life is inseparable from the work, it makes sense to begin there. Born in St. Paul, Minnesota, shortly after the end of World War II, Hampl attended Catholic schools, then the University of Minnesota, where she is now Regents Professor and McKnight Distinguished University Professor. She teaches in the creative writing program there—a program that didn't exist when she was an undergraduate. Except for a two-year stint at the Iowa Writers' Workshop, St. Paul—city of romance, city of churches, city that F. Scott Fitzgerald fled—has always been her home. (To have lived always in the same place is not the same as being a homebody. Hampl travels often and to far-flung destinations. Most of her books could just as easily be shelved with travel books as with memoirs.)

It's almost as if being tied to one place freed her mind to roam. *A Romantic Education* ranges between the geographic poles of her life, St. Paul and Prague. Her father's family is Czech and her book takes her "behind the Iron Curtain." The book records an interior journey too, the story of a mind seeking to connect the ordinary ("I come from people who have always been polite enough to feel that nothing has ever happened to them") to the beautiful ("For the first time I recognized the truth of beauty: it is brokenness, it is on its knees").

Virgin Time, Hampl's second memoir, traces a physical pilgrimage to Assisi, with stops at Lourdes and at a Northern California monastery. The spiritual journey here is one of rediscovery: after turning away from Catholic dogma, she once again opens herself to the mysteries of faith, prayer, and contemplative life.

"Memoir" is an imprecise label for Hampl's next book-length work. Like Mark Doty's *Still Life with Oysters and Lemon,* and her own *Spillville* (her Dvořák book, which she did with the artist Steven Sorman), *Blue Arabesque: A Search for the Sublime* (2006), is sui generis. It revolves around the figure of the reclining female—the odalisque of Western imagination and, in particular, of Matisse's paintings. Here the writing inhabits a liminal space between prose poem, personal essay, memoir, travel writing, and art criticism. In *The New York Times,* Kathryn Harrison calls *Blue Arabesque* "a paean to the act of seeing, celebrating our capacity to be transformed by the truths art holds, recognizing them as…holy." (The ellipsis is Harrison's, its effect to delay, then emphasize the word "holy.")

Hampl's most recent memoir is also the most traditional, formally speaking. *The Florist's Daughter* is storytelling in the old-fashioned sense: people—mainly her tart-tongued mother, who worked as a library file clerk, and her gentle florist father—move through space and time. The title both complicates and comments on the book's biggest revelation. "In a sense," Hampl says, "the title is a gentle irony: I *thought* I was my father's daughter, but in fact…"

When the book opens, Stan Hampl has been dead for several years, and Mary is dying. Ever dutiful, ever the writer, Patricia holds her mother's unconscious hand with her own right hand while scribbling an obituary with her left. From that scene, she loops back to her parents' courtship and marriage, then forward to their children (Patricia has an older brother, Peter), and their first home, an apartment on Banfil Street; then their second home, on Linwood, farther from the Old World of the Czech relatives and closer to the grandees of St. Paul society, who dwelt (where else?) on Summit Avenue. From an early age, Hampl's ears were tuned to the frequency of the unspoken. "Terrible oddities abrade[d] our peaceful world," Hampl writes. Among them, the bowdlerized version told to young Patricia of the girlhood rape of an aunt *(It was an* almost *rape!)*; there was her mother's epilepsy; there was the Czech grandmother who couldn't write English; there was, finally, a marriage that, if not blissful, couldn't be described as unhappy, though it grew vexed as her parents aged.

Mostly, though, *The Florist's Daughter* concerns itself with the numinous ordinary, what Don DeLillo calls "the radiance of dailiness." Hampl's mother was a storyteller, hoarder of details, "a veritable Proust of the breakfast table," possessed of a keen eye and a knack for "reading a scene from the gestures of minor characters." Though Hampl's father never thought of himself as an artist, his floral arrangements were perpetually in demand for weddings and funerals and society balls. After plying "his magic box of color and light," Stan would stand with Mary in the anterooms of great twinkling houses, watching the wealthy at play. "She was tracking," writes their daughter. "He was filled with wonder."

Hailing *The Florist's Daughter* as Hampl's best memoir yet, Danielle Trussoni writes in *The New York Times*, "Her signature literary triangulations—the author analyzing herself as she explicates the world through artists she worships—dissolve in the emotional immediacy of her subject...[H]er own life takes front and center stage. The result is electric and alive."

Like Mary McCarthy's *Memories of a Catholic Girlhood* and Annie Dillard's *An American Childhood*, Hampl's memoirs tell the story of a writer in the making. What are the particular, peculiar forces that shaped her? For one, the sense that she was never quite at the center but always on the outside looking in—feeling, as F. Scott Fitzgerald did, poor (or at least middle class) in a rich man's town. And she was shaped by an early hunch that the ordinary was a worthy subject for literature. (In this respect, she's given courage and direction to a generation of memoirists cursed with happy childhoods.) In her dual roles as scribe and troublemaker, Hampl found a way to reconcile her mother's hungry eye for detail with her father's capacity for awe. The memoirist tracks, she is filled with wonder.

Along with personal narrative, Hampl writes stories and poems and even spoken-word presentations, which she has performed to musical accompaniment by Dan Chouinard, her partner in these "staged essays" produced by Minnesota Public Radio and available on its Web site. Her work—including essays and journalism—has appeared in *The New Yorker, The Paris Review, The New York Times, Los Angeles Times, Best American Short Stories,* and *Best American Essays. The New York Times Book Review* has named four of Hampl's titles to its "Notable Books" of the year lists. *I Could Tell You Stories* was a finalist for the National Book Critics Circle Award in General Nonfiction in 2000. *The Florist's Daughter* won the 2008 Minnesota Book Award for Memoir and Creative Nonfiction. Hampl is coeditor, with the eminent American cultural historian Elaine Tyler May, of *Tell Me True: Memoir, History, and Writing a Life,* a collection of essays by memoirists, including Hampl and May. The recipient of a MacArthur fellowship (the so-called "genius grant"), Hampl has also received fellowships from the Guggenheim Foundation, Bush Foundation, National Endowment for the Arts (twice, once in poetry, and once in prose), Ingram Merrill Foundation, and Djerassi Foundation. She was a Fulbright Fellow to Prague shortly after the end of the Cold War. Along with other distinguished alumni of the Iowa Writers' Workshop, she has her name and a fragment of her writing in concrete on an Iowa City sidewalk: "Maybe being oneself is always an acquired taste."

Hampl's essay collection, *I Could Tell You Stories,* marked her arrival as one of the most eloquent and elegant *theorists* of the memoir, which she calls "the quest literature of our times." What a strange and paradoxical form memoir is, a creature neither of earth nor air, inhabiting, as Hampl writes, "the indeterminate narrative space between fiction and documentary." The memoir does not merely transcribe events but shapes them as well. It grants itself permission to show *and* tell. Like lyric poetry, memoir cavorts through time and space, trailing its long ribbon of associations. Above all, memoir converts the personal self, that ostensible subject, into nothing more (or less) than a tool of perception. The memoirist's quarry is always larger, more durable, and more multifaceted than what it seems initially to be. "True memoir is written, like all literature, in an attempt to find not only a self but a world," writes Hampl. The pleasures of memoir writing, one senses from reading her, are not the superficial, fleeting pleasures of self-indulgence. They are the deep, enduring joys of transcending the self, of creating a world out of words. "To write one's life is to live it twice," says Hampl, "and the second living is both spiritual and historical, for a memoir reaches deep within the personality as it seeks its narrative form and it also grasps the life-of-the-times as no political analysis can."

Hampl's writing often springs from a detail or image, what she calls "the spongy thinginess of life." The metaphor brings to mind those brightly colored capsules that children love. Dropped in a bowl of warm water, each one blossoms into a surprise creature: a purple elephant, a blue brontosaurus, an orange snow leopard. Hampl might begin, say, with an image of a young woman—her former self—

captivated by a Matisse painting, or with a scene glimpsed through the blurry window of a Greyhound bus taking that same young woman to visit her boyfriend in prison, where he is serving a sentence for draft resistance. Under the fierce light of the memoirist's gaze, the image accordions out into a form capacious enough to hold everything—art, politics, religion, travel, photography, reading, writing, inspiration ("the one bit of God we haven't managed to kill off")—on which her supple mind alights. Hampl's writing surprises with lightning shifts in texture or in tone, with sly or wry asides enclosed in parentheses or dashes. The architecture she likes best is an eclectic, electric mix of high and low, swerves and lines, past and present, political and personal; things she read in a book ("What gives value to travel is fear": Camus) and a tossed-off response from a former boyfriend's mother: "That is the sort of observation Katherine Mansfield made."

Hampl's impulses are essayistic in the Montaignian sense. She is always making a run at something, peeling back the layers of her defenses, seeking the nimbleness of mind needed to get her over one hurdle or another, to see the connection between seemingly disparate things. Hampl, like all essayists, keeps *trying* in the face of strong odds and only the faintest whiff of success. As T. S. Eliot says, in the end, "there is only the trying."

The world often strikes her as simultaneously serious and absurd. (*The Florist's Daughter* could just as easily have been titled *The Daughter of Retail Sales,* she joked to Diane Rehm.) It seems deeply mysterious. It knocks her off her pins, throws her for a loop, unmoors her occasionally. Most of the time, she dwells comfortably in uncertainty (which is not to say the writing is ever less than sure-footed). The voice speaking from her pages is smart but never show-offy. It is rigorously unsentimental. ("You can't be a writer and believe everything," she told Rehm. "You have to have that little ice chip in your heart.") She is full of Midwestern modesty but not self-deprecation—or, heaven forbid, the buffoonery of the writer who thinks the only way to woo readers is by making them laugh at him. ("To say less of yourself than is true is stupidity, not modesty," writes Montaigne.) The voice whispering in our ear is that of a clear-eyed, sympathetic, and above all wise friend who craves not our laughter or applause (though she wins both) but our *conversation*.

Is one ever tempted to ask what became of the young woman who once predicted she would write fiction "from now on"? Perhaps. Then again, perhaps the answer is obvious: She simply acquired a taste for being herself.

Jennifer Brice is the author of Unlearning to Fly *and* The Last Settlers. *Her writing has appeared* The Gettysburg Review, River Teeth, Manoa, Under the Sun, The Dolphin Reader, *and* American Nature Writing, *among others. She teaches at Colgate University.*

REAL ESTATE
A Plan B Essay by Terese Svoboda

> In the Plan B essay series, writers discuss their contingency plans, extra-literary passions, and the roads not traveled.

My father always wanted me to go into real estate. It was in the family: pioneer land swaps and strategic purchases during the Depression kept the Svobodas solvent. My father would stand at the edge of one of his huge blank fields and proclaim his ownership: All of this! Then four antelope would gallop across the horizon and just before they'd disappear, he'd point at them and say that's where the land ended. Once he managed to amass four thousand acres of contiguous field, a great feat in the cutup map that the West is made of, but it didn't last long—he soon traded it for something else.

I bought my first country house out of the back of the *Village Voice* for $8,000, rehabbing it with my husband and selling it for twice the price. The buyer brought cash in a suitcase. My husband and I spent the next ten years wrestling an artist's loft out of the City of New York, no mean real estate feat. Advertised with a purchase price of $1, the Lower East Side tenement building had no floors or roof, and a tree grew through the foundation. Five years into the rehab, the City, noticing real estate values skyrocketing, slapped a very large lien on the deal. We dealt anyway. When we had to move to Silicon Valley during its insane heyday, we were told there were no houses in our modest price range. We found one, for sale by owner, and bought it ten minutes after we walked in. Two years later, potential buyers entered a glass room where we listened to their pleading to buy the property, each outbidding the next.

My father still speaks wistfully of a cousin whose daughter is San Francisco's leading realtor. The best I could do, aside from housing myself, was to use my writing to try to capture some of that awe of the land he so cares about.

On the other hand, maybe I did go into real estate.

Terese Svoboda has published fourteen books of poetry, fiction, memoir, and translation.

POSTSCRIPTS
Contest Results · Awards · Dedications · Fall 2012

Emerging Writer's Contest Since 1971, Ploughshares has been committed to promoting the work of up-and-coming writers. After last year's inaugural fiction contest, this was our first year accepting submissions in all three genres—poetry, nonfiction, and fiction. We are pleased to announce the following winners and runners-up. The winners will each receive $1,000 and be published in the Winter 2012-13 issue, edited by John Skoyles and Ladette Randolph.

FICTION
Winner: Jasmine Sawers, "The Culling"
   First Runner Up: Lucinda Nelson Dhavan, "Embracing the Moon"
   Second Runner Up: Neil Fischer, "Yucatán Boy"

POETRY
Winner: Jen Silverman: Five Bath Poems
   First Runner Up: Christine Adams: "Luminous Matter," "Gulping: A Pastoral," "Elegy for the Giant Pacific Octopus," and "Mono Lake, California"
   Second Runner Up: T. J. McLemore: "Dream for the Eve of My Father's Death," "The Mad Miner," "Surfaces Reflect Things," and "F.B.C."

NONFICTION
Winner: Jacob Newberry, "What You Will Do"
   First Runner Up: Kerri Power, "Belief in Evolution"
   Second Runner Up: Suzanne Farrell Smith, "The Pearl"

Many thanks to all of the authors for sharing their work with us. The Emerging Writer's Contest is open to all writers who have yet to publish a book, and is open for submissions from February 1 to April 2. Please visit our Web site (pshares.org) for guidelines, and we look forward to reading your work.

Awards Our congratulations to the following *Ploughshares* writers, whose work has been selected for these anthologies:

Best Stories Angela Pneuman's "Occupational Hazard," from the Spring 2011 issue, edited by Colm Tóibín, and Jennifer Haigh's "Paramour," from the Winter 2011-12 issue, edited by Alice Hoffman, will both be included in *The Best American Short Stories 2012*. The anthology is due out October 2012, with Tom Perrotta as the guest editor and Heidi Pitlor as the series editor.

Best Essays Ewa Hryniewicz-Yarbrough's "Objects of Affection," from the Spring 2011 issue, edited by Colm Tóibín, has been selected for *The Best American Essays 2012*. The anthology is due out October 2012, with David Brooks as the guest editor and Robert Atwan as the series editor.

Best Poetry Michael Morse's "Void and Compensation (Facebook)," from the Spring 2011 issue, edited by Colm Tóibín, has been selected for *The Best American Poetry 2012*. The anthology is due out September 2012, with Mark Doty as the guest editor and David Lehman as the series editor.

Pushcart Bruce Bennett's "The Thing's Impossible" and Jane Hirshfield's "In a Kitchen Where Mushrooms Were Washed," both from the Fall 2011 issue, edited by DeWitt Henry, have been selected for *The Pushcart Prize XXXVII: Best of the Small Presses*, which is due out on November 2012 from Bill Henderson's Pushcart Press.

Guest Editor Dedications

Carl H. Klaus is a diarist and essayist, and a specialist in nonfiction writing. He was founding director of the University of Iowa's Nonfiction Writing Program, and is professor emeritus at Iowa, where he co-edits Sightline Books: The Iowa Series in Literary Nonfiction. His books include *My Vegetable Love* and its companion *Weathering Winter,* as well as *Taking Retirement: A Beginner's Diary* and *Letters to Kate: Life after Life,* essayistic works that reflect on his life and marriage, gardening and food, work and retirement, and his concern with time, change, and mortality. His latest books are *The Made-Up Self: Impersonation in the Personal Essay,* and the co-edited collection, *Essayists on the Essay: Four Centuries of Commentary.*

David Hamilton is a memoirist and essayist, and an influential literary editor. He is Professor of English at the University of Iowa where he teaches medieval literature (his early training) across a wide range of interests into modern and contemporary writing, especially the essay and lyric poetry. From 1977 until 2009 he was the editor of *The Iowa Review,* sustaining it as one of America's premier literary journals and a welcome home to literary and personal essays. His special interest as an essayist and scholar is Montaigne. His own works include *Deep River: A Memoir of a Missouri Farm, Textualities: Essays on Poetry in the United States,* and *Ossabaw,* a collection of poems.

NOTES ON NEIHARDT
A Look2 Essay by Barry Gifford

> The Look2 essay series, which replaces our print book reviews, takes a closer look at the careers of accomplished authors who have yet to receive the full appreciation that their work deserves. Reviews of new books can still be found on our blog at blog.pshares.org.

It was my good fortune to have been enrolled in a class called "Twilight of the Sioux" at the University of Missouri in 1964, taught by the Nebraska poet John Neihardt. I was seventeen years old and at Missouri to play baseball and football. "Twilight of the Sioux" was a one-unit course recommended by the athletic department to so-called scholar-athletes because the instructor was well known for liberally handing out As, and was therefore a boon to shoring up athletes' grade point averages in order to keep them eligible to play.

I knew nothing about Neihardt, but I had spotted him on my first day on campus in Columbia, Missouri, a tiny old guy barely five feet tall, wearing a Homburg-style hat, wire-rim glasses, and a three-piece suit. He was bending down to sniff flowers growing alongside the sidewalks. This gentle-appearing little man seemed to me a curious figure, an anomaly among the fast-moving students and faculty members rushing around on their way to and from classes. Neihardt took his time, and I liked that.

In class, Neihardt spoke softly and with great passion and reverence for the Plains Indians: the Sioux, Cheyenne, and Arapaho. I was ignorant of his having authored *Black Elk Speaks,* basically a transcription of the words of an Oglala Sioux holy man, first published in 1932; it was on the Pine Ridge Reservation that the name Flaming Rainbow was bestowed upon Neihardt. In the late 1960s, this book became a kind of sacred text for a new generation interested in Native American history and the notion of "getting back to the land." *Black Elk Speaks* continues to be a popular title to this day.

The other students in my class barely paid attention to Neihardt's lectures; they were there for the grade and were mostly biding their time until team practice. But I was fascinated by his narratives of having lived and moved among those last survivors of the ethnic cleansing perpetrated by predominantly white "settlers" and the United States Army operating according to the mandate of manifest destiny. Neihardt did not disparage this business of "civilizing" the West, but he did talk about the need to preserve the knowledge inherent in Native American cultures and to study their manners of survival. "Twilight of the Sioux" and *Black Elk Speaks* were inspired by Neihardt's interest in the Plains Indians' belief in the coming of a messiah to restore their lands to them during the mid-1880s, which resulted in what the U.S. government deemed a rebellion that ended violently at Wounded Knee on December 29, 1890.

I left Missouri in early May of 1965, but I never forgot Neihardt. A few years later, I read his *A Cycle of the West,* five narrative poems originally published between 1915 and 1949; one of them, "The Song of the Indian Wars," he had read aloud in our class. I also read *When the Tree Flowered* (1951), a fictional biography of Eagle Voice, a Sioux Indian; *The River and I* (1938), a compilation of a series of articles Neihardt wrote for *Outing Magazine* in 1910 about a trip he made down the Missouri River in 1908; and, of course, *Black Elk Speaks.*

Neihardt chose to record many of his histories in the form of poetry, using a type of verse derided by the determined modernist Ezra Pound, who declared, in 1908 or so, that it was poetry such as John Neihardt's, celebrated by ladies' tearoom societies, that caused him to leave the country. Following his graduation from the University of Pennsylvania,

Pound taught at Wabash College, a position from which he was fired for allowing a burlesque performer to sleep in his room—on the floor, he said. He soon embarked for Venice, Italy, and upon his arrival there proclaimed it, "a fine place to come to from Crawfordsville, Indiana."

Pound, of course, along with T. S. Eliot, William Carlos Williams, and James Joyce, among others, quickly eclipsed Neihardt and his fellow practitioners whose work was favored by those gathering in tearooms; but it was the poetry and criticism of Eliot, before and after his receiving tutelage and guidance from Pound, that did much to establish, for better or worse, the foundation of English departments in American universities. It is unlikely that the poetry of John Neihardt is today considered an essential part of curricula in literature classes.

I saw Neihardt being interviewed on television, in 1970, I believe, by the talk show host Dick Cavett. Like Neihardt, Cavett was a Nebraskan (though Neihardt was born in Illinois)—the interview took place in Lincoln—and Neihardt, who held the post of Poet Laureate of Nebraska from 1921 until his death in 1973 at the age of ninety-two, had become something of a mini-celebrity owing to the popularity of *Black Elk Speaks.* By then it had become a hippie handbook, outselling even Jack Kerouac's *On the Road.* I don't remember much about the interview other than that the old poet looked much the same as when I had encountered him in Columbia, Missouri, where he was still teaching and where he eventually died. I recall that Neihardt often wore a little flower freshly picked on his morning walk.

Ezra Pound was a great teacher, not only for T. S. Eliot but, through his books *The Spirit of Romance, Guide to Kulchur, The ABC of Reading,* the anthology *Confucius to Cummings,* and his *Cantos,* for me and by now tens of thousands of others. But so was John Neihardt, not as a great poet, perhaps, but as a personal historian of a time and place and culture that without his interest and diligence would certainly be less well understood and appreciated. What's more, I don't recall Neihardt ever having said a bad word about Ezra Pound.

Barry Gifford's fiction, nonfiction, and poetry have been published in twenty-eight languages. His books Sailor's Holiday *(Random House, 1991) and* The Phantom Father *(Harcourt Brace, 1997) were each* named a Notable Book of the Year by the New York Times, and his book Wyoming *(Arcade Publishing, 2000) was named a Novel of the Year by the Los Angeles Times. His film credits include* Wild at Heart, Perdita Durango, Lost Highway, City of Ghosts, Ball Lightning, *and* The Phantom Father. *Barry Gifford's most recent books are* Sailor & Lula: The Complete Novels *(Seven Stories Press, 2010) and* Sad Stories of the Death of Kings *(Seven Stories Press, 2010). He lives in the San Francisco Bay Area. For more information visit www.BarryGifford.com.*

EDITORS' SHELF
Book Recommendations from Our Advisory Editors

DeWitt Henry recommends Doug Crandell's *They're Calling You Home:* "In Crandell's fourth novel, a memoirist is exiled for exposing family secrets, but in returning home to research a true crime book, he re-embraces his family and confronts life's inscrutable evils, along with its demands for love and charity. A novel to celebrate." (Northern Illinois University Press, 2012)

Tony Hoagland recommends *How Literature Saved My Life: Essays by David Shields:* "Shields is the Raskolnikov, or maybe the Rumpelstiltskin, of American nonfiction; his restless, economical essays thread a path between ironic oddity and sincerity, between postmodern Jeremiad (denunciations of contemporary fiction and its boring moralistic conventions, an essay about his resemblance to George Bush) and confessional nakedness. He's fierce and interesting about contemporary writing and how it fits in with, attacks, or negotiates contemporary reality. Many pieces here depart as 'appreciations' of other artists, then dive into the personal. Never boring." (Knopf, February 2013)

Philip Levine recommends *Stealing History* by Gerald Stern: "Who knew Stern could write such rich and saucy prose? The format, 84 entries in his mental and spiritual journal of the year 2010—the year he turned 84—allows him to cover so many of his interests, his loyalties, his angers, his beliefs, his several histories, his loves. Jesus Christ is here, as are Paul McCartney, Henry Miller, Larry Levis, and his neighbor Charlie, half-brother of Humphrey Bogart. And of course the poets and their work. He remembers his early years as a teacher, as well as his Iowa years. It's astounding how much he's read and how much he remembers, and he has an attitude toward everything. This is a profound and hilarious book." (Trinity University Press, January 2012)

David St. John recommends *When the Only Light Is Fire* by Saeed Jones: "This extraordinary debut chapbook contains poems that are bruised by a carnal grace. The exquisite—even elegant—music of this work and its dark psychosexual dynamics combine to make this one of the most exciting collections I've read this year." (Sibling Rivalry Press, 2011)

EDITORS' CORNER
New Works by Our Advisory Editors

Richard Ford, *Canada,* a novel (Ecco, June 2012)

Don Lee, *The Collective,* a novel (Norton, May 2012)

Christopher Tilghman, *The Right-Hand Stone,* a novel (Farrar, Straus and Giroux, May 2012)

CONTRIBUTORS' NOTES
Fall 2012

Charles Baxter is the author of twelve books of fiction and nonfiction. Pantheon published his most recent collection, *Gryphon: New and Selected Stories*, in 2011. Vintage has just reissued his novel *First Light*, from 1987. He lives in Minneapolis and teaches at the University of Minnesota.

Kelly Grey Carlisle's essays have appeared in *River Teeth, Subtropics, Tampa Review, Waccamaw,* and *The Touchstone Anthology of Contemporary Creative Nonfiction*. She teaches writing at Trinity University in San Antonio, Texas.

Robert Clark is the author of ten books: the novels *In the Deep Midwinter* (Picador, 1997), *Mr. White's Confession* (Picador, 1998), *Love Among the Ruins* (Norton, 2001), *The Lives of the Artists* (Harper Collins, 2005), and *Heaven* (just published, CreateSpace, 2012), as well as the nonfiction works *River of the West* (Harper Collins, 1995), *The Solace of Food* (Steerforth, 1998), *My Grandfather's House* (Picador, 1999), *Dark Water: Flood and Redemption in the City of Masterpieces* (Doubleday, 2008), and, most recently, *Bayham Street: Essays in Longing* (CreateSpace, 2012). He is a winner of the Edgar for Best Novel, the Washington State Book Award, and a Guggenheim Fellowship in Creative Non-Fiction. He lives in Seattle.

Jennifer De Leon is the winner of the 2011 *Fourth Genre* Michael Steinberg Essay Prize. Her work has appeared in *Ms., Briar Cliff Review, Poets & Writers, Guernica, The Best Women's Travel Writing 2010,* and elsewhere. A member of the Macondo Writers' Workshop, she has been awarded scholarships and residencies from the Bread Loaf Writers' Conference, Hedgebrook, and the Vermont Studio Center. She is the editor of the anthology *Wise Latina* (University of Nebraska Press, 2013), and she is working on a novel.

Patricia Foster is the author of the memoir *All the Lost Girls* (University of Alabama Press, 2000), winner of the PEN/Jerard Award; *Just Beneath My Skin* (University of Georgia, 2004), essays; and the forthcoming novel *Girls from Soldier Creek*, winner of the Fred Bonnie Award. She is the editor of *Minding the Body: Women Writers on Body and Soul; Sister to Sister;* and the forthcoming *Understanding the Essay* (coedited with Jeff Porter). Foster has been a professor in the MFA Program in Nonfiction at the University of Iowa for nineteen years, has been an exchange professor in Montpellier, France, and has taught in Prague, Melbourne, Wollongong, Barcelona, and Florence.

Lynn Freed's work has appeared in *The New Yorker, Harper's, The Atlantic Monthly, Southwest Review, The Georgia Review, The New York Times, The Washington Post, The Wall Street Journal, National Geographic,* and

Narrative Magazine, among other publications. She is the recipient of numerous awards, including the inaugural Katherine Anne Porter Award from the American Academy of Arts and Letters, a PEN/O. Henry Award, fellowships, and grants and support from the National Endowment for the Arts and The Guggenheim Foundation. Born in South Africa, she now lives in Northern California.

Mary Gordon is the author of six previous novels, two memoirs, a short-story collection, and *Reading Jesus* (Pantheon, 2009), a work of nonfiction. She has received many honors, including a Lila Wallace—Reader's Digest Writers' Award, a Guggenheim Fellowship, an O. Henry Award, an Academy Award for Literature from the American Academy of Arts and Letters, and the Story Prize. She is the State Writer of New York. Gordon teaches at Barnard College and lives in New York City.

L. K. Hanson is a graphic artist and writer from Minneapolis, where he worked for the *Star Tribune,* Minnesota's largest daily. He is a graduate of St. Olaf College, where he was artist-in-residence. He has taught illustration and lettering at the College of Visual Arts in St. Paul, and has illustrated books for Workman Publishing and the Hazelden Foundation. Hanson is now in semiretirement, and his work appears weekly on the *Star Tribune*'s opinion page.

Phillip Lopate is the author of more than a dozen titles, including *Waterfront* (Crown, 2004), *Portrait of My Body* (Doubleday, 1996), and *Notes on Sontag* (Princeton University Press, 2009). His forthcoming books are *Essay Love* (personal essays) and *To Show and to Tell: The Craft of Literary Nonfiction,* both from The Free Press/Simon & Schuster in March 2013. He directs Columbia University's graduate nonfiction program.

Nancy Lord, a former Alaska Writer Laureate, is the author of three short fiction and five literary nonfiction books, including most recently *Early Warming: Crisis and Response in the Climate-Changed North* (Counterpoint Press, 2011). She teaches part-time for the University of Alaska and is currently working on a novel set among ocean scientists and controversy in a near future.

David Stuart MacLean lives in Chicago. He earned his PhD in Literature and Creative Writing from the University of Houston and his MFA from New Mexico State University. He was named 2011's best Emerging Nonfiction Writer by the PEN American Foundation. His work has appeared in *Quarterly West, Gulf Coast, Guernica,* and the radio program *This American Life.* His memoir, *The Answer to the Riddle Is Me,* will be published by Houghton Mifflin Harcourt in 2013.

Thomas Mallon is the author of eight novels, including *Henry and*

Clara (Houghton Mifflin, 1994), *Fellow Travelers* (Pantheon, 2007), and the recently published *Watergate* (Pantheon, 2012). His nonfiction books include *Yours Ever: People and Their Letters* (Pantheon, 2009), *Mrs. Paine's Garage* (Pantheon, 2002), *Stolen Words* (Ticknor & Fields, 1989), and *A Book of One's Own* (Ticknor & Fields, 1984). His writing appears in *The New Yorker, The New York Times Book Review,* and *The Atlantic.* He lives in Washington, D.C., and directs the creative writing program at The George Washington University.

Kimberly Meyer's work appears in *The Best American Travel Writing 2012* (October, 2012) and *The Kenyon Review* (August, 2012), and has appeared in *Ecotone; The Oxford American; The Georgia Review; AGNI; The Southern Review; Brain, Child; Crab Orchard Review; Natural Bridge;* and *Third Coast.* Currently she teaches in a Great Books program in the Honors College at the University of Houston. She is also at work on a book about the journey she and her daughter recently completed, in which they retraced the medieval pilgrimage route of Felix Fabri, a Dominican friar from Germany, who traveled to the Holy Land and St. Catherine's Monastery in the Sinai Desert in 1483.

Eileen Pollack's most recent novel, *Breaking and Entering* (Four Way Books, 2012), was awarded the 2012 Grub Street National Book Prize and named a *New York Times* Editor's Choice selection; *In the Mouth: Stories and Novellas* (Four Way Books, 2008) won the 2008 Edward Lewis Wallant Award. Her essays have appeared in many periodicals, including *The New York Times,* and she is the author of *Creative Nonfiction: A Guide to Form, Content, and Style, with Readings.* She teaches on the faculty of the MFA Program at the University of Michigan.

Ralph James Savarese is the author of *Reasonable People: A Memoir of Autism and Adoption* (Other Press, 2007). He is also the coeditor of "The Lyrical Body," a special issue of *Seneca Review,* and of *Papa PhD: Essays on Fatherhood by Men in the Academy* (Rutgers University Press, 2010). His creative work has appeared, among other places, in *New England Review, Fourth Genre, Stone Canoe, Southwest Review, Sewanee Review,* and *Seneca Review.* He teaches at Grinnell College.

Dani Shapiro is the author of the memoirs *Devotion* (Harper, 2010) and *Slow Motion* (Random House, 1998), and five novels, including *Black & White* (Anchor, 2008) and *Family History* (Knopf, 2003). Her work has appeared in *The New Yorker, Granta, Tin House, One Story, n+1, Vogue, Elle,* and *The New York Times Book Review.* This is her second appearance in *Ploughshares.* She has taught most recently in the graduate writing program at Brooklyn College. Her new book, *Still Writing,* will be published by Grove/Atlantic in 2013.

Mark Slouka's books, which have been translated into sixteen languages, include a collection of stories, *Lost Lake* (Knopf, 1998); the novels *God's Fool* (Knopf, 2002) and *The Visible World* (Houghton Mifflin Harcourt, 2007); and *Essays from the Nick of Time* (Graywolf, 2010). His new novel, *Brewster,* will be coming out with W. W. Norton. He and his family may be living in Arizona next year.

Xu Xi (許 素 細) is the author of nine books of fiction and essays, including *Access: Thirteen Tales* (Signal 8 Press, 2011); the novel *Habit of a Foreign Sky* (Haven Books, 2010), a finalist for the inaugural Man Asian Literary Prize; and an essay collection, *Evanescent Isles* (Hong Kong University Press, 2008). From 2009 to 2012, she served as MFA Faculty Chair at Vermont College of Fine Arts. She is Writer-in-Residence at the Department of English, City University of Hong Kong, where she established and directs an international, low-residency MFA in creative writing, the first to focus specifically on Asia. Her Web site is www.xuxiwriter.com.

GUEST EDITOR POLICY

Ploughshares is published three times a year: mixed issues of poetry and prose in the spring and winter and a prose issue in the fall, with each guest-edited by a different writer of prominence. Guest editors are invited to solicit up to half of their issues, with the other half selected from unsolicited manuscripts screened for them by staff editors. This guest editor policy is designed to introduce readers to different literary circles and tastes, and to offer a fuller representation of the range and diversity of contemporary letters than would be possible with a single editorship. Yet, at the same time, we expect every issue to reflect our overall standards of literary excellence.

SUBMISSION POLICIES

We welcome unsolicited manuscripts from June 1 to January 15 (postmark dates). All submissions postmarked from January 16 to May 31 will be returned unread. Submit your work at any time during our reading period; if a manuscript is not timely for one issue, it will be considered for another.

Our backlog is unpredictable, and staff editors ultimately have the responsibility of determining for which editor a work is most appropriate. We accept submissions online. Please see our Web site (www.pshares.org) for more information and guidelines. Unsolicited work sent directly to a guest editor's home or office will be ignored and discarded. All mailed manuscripts and correspondence regarding submissions should be accompanied by a self-addressed, stamped envelope (s.a.s.e.). No replies will be given by e-mail (exceptions are made for international submissions). Expect three to five months for a decision. We now receive well over a thousand manuscripts a month.

For prose that is significantly longer than 5,000 words, we are now accepting submissions for *Pshares Singles*, which will be published as e-books. *Singles* can stretch to novella length, and can range from 6,000 to 25,000 words. The series will be edited by Ladette Randolph, *Ploughshares* editor-in-chief.

Simultaneous submissions are fine as long as they are indicated as such and we are notified immediately upon acceptance elsewhere. We do not reprint previously published work. Translations are welcome if permission has been granted. We cannot be responsible for delay, loss, or damage. Payment is upon publication: $25/printed page, $50 minimum and $250 maximum per author, with two copies of the issue and a one-year subscription. For *Pshares Singles*, payment is $250 for long stories and $500 for work that is closer to a novella.

PLOUGHSHARES
LITERARY MAGAZINE

Did you know that we have a regularly updated blog with posts about writing and publishing from guest bloggers featured in this issue, plus book reviews and news?

Join us online:
Blog: blog.pshares.org
Website: pshares.org
Stay connected:
Tweet @Pshares
Facebook.com/Ploughshares

Also available on

BENNINGTON WRITING SEMINARS

MFA in Writing and Literature
Two-Year Low-Residency Program

Read one hundred books. Write one.

NEW

Annual Liam Rector Poetry Prize
(Open to all current graduating Writing Seminars poets)

FICTION ♦ NONFICTION POETRY

Partial Scholarships Available
Bennington College Writing Seminars
One College Drive
Bennington, VT 05201
802-440-4452
www.bennington.edu/MFAWriting

FOUNDER • Liam Rector
DIRECTOR • Sven Birkerts
CORE FACULTY

FICTION
Martha Cooley
David Gates
Amy Hempel
Bret Anthony Johnston
Sheila Kohler
Alice Mattison
Askold Melnyczuk
Brian Morton
Rachel Pastan
Lynne Sharon Schwartz
Paul Yoon

NONFICTION
Sven Birkerts
Susan Cheever
Bernard Cooper
Dinah Lenney
Phillip Lopate

POETRY
April Bernard
Amy Gerstler
Major Jackson
Timothy Liu
Ed Ochester
Mark Wunderlich

WRITERS-IN-RESIDENCE
Lyndall Gordon
Donald Hall
Rick Moody
Bob Shacochis

PAST FACULTY IN RESIDENCE
André Aciman
Douglas Bauer
Frank Bidart
Tom Bissell
Amy Bloom
Lucie Brock-Broido
Wesley Brown
Peter Campion
Henri Cole
Elizabeth Cox
Robert Creeley
Nicholas Delbanco
Stephen Dobyns
Mark Doty
Stephen Dunn
Thomas Sayers Ellis
Katie Ford
Lynn Freed
Mary Gaitskill
Vivian Gornick
Barry Hannah
Jane Hirshfield
Jane Kenyon
Michael Krüger
David Lehman
Barry Lopez
Thomas Lynch
Valerie Martin
Jill McCorkle
E. Ethelbert Miller
Sue Miller
Paul Muldoon
Howard Norman
George Packer
Carl Phillips
Jayne Anne Phillips
Robert Pinsky
Francine Prose
Lia Purpura
David Shields
Jason Shinder
Tree Swenson
Larissa Szporluk
Wells Tower
Rosanna Warren
James Wood

$5,000 Miller Williams Arkansas Poetry Prize

Submissions accepted in September and October, 2012. One winner and up to three finalists will be published in 2014.

In addition to publication, the winner will receive the $5,000 Miller Williams Arkansas Poetry Prize.

The series is open to all book-length manuscripts by a single author of 60 to 90 pages, except translations. Send your manuscript and reading fee ($25) to:

The Miller Williams Arkansas Poetry Prize
University of Arkansas Press
105 N. McIlroy Ave.
Fayetteville, AR 72701

For more information see www.uapress.com

2012 Winner and Finalists

The University of Arkansas Press

www.uapress.com • 800-626-0090
facebook.com/uarkpress • twitter.com/uarkpress

Layovers just got a lot more literary

THE KENYON REVIEW
Now available on the **amazon**kindle

time	space	support
3 years	*Austin*	*$27,500 per year*

MFA IN WRITING

THE MICHENER CENTER FOR WRITERS
The University of Texas at Austin

www.utexas.edu/academic/mcw
512-471-1601

SANTA MONICA *Review*

fall 2012

available now

Fictions & Essays
Victoria Patterson / Gary Fincke
Mary Jones / Soo Yeon Hong
Brendan Park / Debbie Urbanski / Tara Scalzo
Venita Blackburn / Rav Grewal-Kök
Sean Bernard / Dave Kim / Diane Lefer
Cover: Fred Lonidier

$7 copy / **$12** yr. subscription
SM Review / Santa Monica College
1900 Pico Blvd. / Santa Monica, CA 90405
www.smc.edu/sm_review

NAMED ONE OF THE 10 BEST LITERARY MAGAZINES IN NEW ENGLAND

reDiVider

redividerjournal.org

PAST CONTRIBUTORS include

George Singleton · Paul Muldoon · Robert Olen Butler · Bob Hicok · Steve Almond · Claudia Emerson · Shelley Jackson · Kelly Link · Billy Collins · Hannah Tinti · Sherman Alexie

PLOUGHSHARES
Stories and poems for literary aficionados

Known for its compelling fiction and poetry, *Ploughshares* is widely regarded as one of America's most influential literary journals. Most issues are guest-edited by a different writer for a fresh, provocative slant—exploring personal visions, aesthetics, and literary circles—and contributors include both well-known and emerging writers. *Ploughshares* has become a premier proving ground for new talent, showcasing the early works of Sue Miller, Edward P. Jones, Tim O'Brien, and countless others. Past guest editors include Richard Ford, Raymond Carver, Derek Walcott, Tobias Wolff, Kathryn Harrison, and Lorrie Moore. This unique editorial format has made *Ploughshares* a dynamic anthology series—one that has established a tradition of quality and prescience. *Ploughshares* is published in April, August, and December, usually with a prose issue in the fall and mixed issues of poetry and fiction in the spring and winter. Inside each issue, you'll find not only great new stories, essays, and poems, but also a profile on the guest editor, book reviews, and miscellaneous notes about *Ploughshares*, its writers, and the literary world. Subscribe today.

Subscribe online at www.pshares.org.

- -

☐ Send me a one-year subscription for $30.
  I save $12 off the cover price (3 issues).

☐ Send me a two-year subscription for $50.
  I save $34 off the cover price (6 issues).

Start with: ☐ Spring ☐ Fall ☐ Winter

Name _____

Address _____

_____

E-mail _____

Mail with check to: Ploughshares · Emerson College
                      120 Boylston St. · Boston, MA 02116

Add $30 per year for international postage ($10 for Canada).